Library of Congress Cataloging in Publication Data

Schlegel, Dorothy B
    James Branch Cabell.

    1. Cabell, James Branch, 1879-1958--Addresses, essays, lectures.
PS3505.A153Z725   813'.5'2   74-51
ISBN 0-87700-210-X

Copyright © 1975 by Dorothy B. Schlegel
All rights reserved.

This edition is limited to 200 copies.

THE REVISIONIST PRESS
G.P.O. Box 2009
Brooklyn, N. Y. 11202

Printed and Bound in the United States of America

JAMES BRANCH CABELL:
THE RICHMOND ICONOCLAST

by

DOROTHY B. SCHLEGEL

THE JAMES BRANCH CABELL SERIES

To my husband, Dr. Marvin W. Schlegel, who suggested Cabell to me as an author worthy of investigation and whose ever-present help and encouragement have made this book possible. Also, to that great lady and excellent typist, Mrs. Dorothy Clark, whose intelligence and support have lent these essays an appearance of uniformity which they otherwise would have woefully lacked. To both of these fine people I wish to extend my thanks and appreciation.

FOREWORD

Many Americans today seem scarcely to have heard of the Virginia writer, James Branch Cabell. The situation was quite different, however, in the 1920's. In that decade his name was on the lips of people as different from each other as Mae West and Carl Van Doren. His popularity, at that time, was caused primarily by the action in 1920 of the New York Society for the Suppression of Vice, which banned his novel <u>Jurgen: A Comedy of Justice</u>, on the grounds of its alleged indecency. Although his name has since faded from view, this Richmond writer continued to produce poems, tales, novels, and essays to the year 1955; in fact, he was still writing busily until his death in 1958, thus closing a writing career which had begun with the publication of <u>The Eagle's Shadow</u>, just after the turn of the century--in 1904.

The major body of Cabell's work was gathered together by the author himself and published in eighteen volumes from 1927 to 1930 under the title <u>The Works of James Branch Cabell</u>. Cabell, however, liked to call his collected works in this edition, "The Biography of the Life of Manuel." After 1930 there were subsequent pieces of work, the most significant of which were classified by Cabell into groups of five separate trilogies. Of these trilogies perhaps the group most worthy of attention from a purely literary standpoint is the trio entitled <u>Smirt</u>, <u>Smith</u>, and <u>Smire</u>, which Cabell called "The Nightmare Has Triplets."

In spite of Cabell's enormous literary output, of some fifty-two volumes, he has largely been ignored by American critics, or, if they have written about him at all, they seem to have been divided completely as to the direction and significance of his work. They have either praised him lavishly or have written the most scathing denunciations of both his person and his books. Perhaps one of the causes for the lack of understanding of Cabell's work is that most American critics have been trained primarily in the Anglo-American literary tradition. Since Cabell did not employ the usual American literary techniques and subject matter, and since his critics found that his works did not seem to conform to the standards which both American and English critics of the twentieth century have come to deem excellent, they have been at a loss as to what to make of him. Many have simply dismissed him as a maverick. In fact, one critic went so far as to say that Cabell had not written in any of the usual literary traditions. Actually, much of Cabell's more mature work is in a definite literary tradition--that of the eighteenth-century Enlightenment, especially the French, although he was influenced to some extent by English and German Enlighteners, such as Pope and Goethe. Cabell had developed catholic tastes in his undergraduate days at William and Mary. During his long life, he had coursed through many literatures and mythologies; consequently, he had become interested in many periods of literature from the Middle Ages to the present. Vestiges of all of these are present in his work, but Cabell usually burst the bubble of any type of illusion which might be termed romantic with a shaft of eighteenth-century scepticism. Although he might, therefore, he considered something of an eclectic, the key to most of his writing is nevertheless to be discovered in the techniques perfected by the Neoclassicists.

Critics, too, have been somewhat divided as to his Weltanschauung. Most have regarded him as a humorist, an opinion which, of course, is supported by Cabell's habit of subtitling his works comedies. However, there is running through most of his work a disturbing sense of the evanescence and pity of life. This double strain, coupled with his invention of other worlds—a device which is of considerable interest to devotees of science fiction—,makes of him a possible and probably unsuspected ancestor of black humorists, such as Kurt Vonnegut, as has been suggested by Robert H. Canary, although Canary does see some significant differences.* The various views which people take of Cabell's work may attest somewhat to his universality, for each reader finds something of himself and of his own interests in Cabell's carefully chiseled passages.

In view of the fact that the essays which follow were originally written at different times with widely different purposes in mind, they have been slightly revised in order to give the group as much continuity as possible under the circumstances. Perhaps they will

*Robert H. Canary, "Whatever Happened to the Cabell Revival?" Kalki, ed. William L. Godshalk (Cincinnati, Ohio: James Branch Cabell Society, 1974) VI, No. 2, 56-57.

throw some light on this complex and many faceted writer and will help to create a renewed interest in him.

Dorothy B. Schlegel

Virginia Beach, 1974, exactly fifty-six years after Cabell finished Beyond Life in the same town "during the atrociously hot August of 1918."

TABLE OF CONTENTS

                                                             Page

FOREWORD   iii

I.   JAMES BRANCH CABELL AND SOUTHERN ROMANTICISM   1

      Presented originally as a lecture in the Institute of Southern Culture series at Longwood College, Farmville, Virginia, 1958. Published in The South in Perspective, ed. Francis B. Simkins (Farmville, Virginia: Longwood College, 1959), pp. 31-48. Reprinted in Southern Writers: Appraisals in Our Time, ed. R. C. Simonini, Jr. (Charlottesville: The University of Virginia Press, 1964), pp. 124-141.

II.   JAMES BRANCH CABELL: A LATTER-DAY ENLIGHTENER   19

      Presented as a paper before the College Language Association, Durham, N. C., 1968. Published by Therman B. O'Daniel, ed., in the CLA Journal, XII, No. 3 (March, 1969), 223-236.

III.   CABELL AND HIS CRITICS   33

      Presented as a lecture in the Institute of Southern Culture series at Longwood College, Farmville, Virginia, 1961. Published in The Dilemma of the Southern Writer, ed. Richard K. Meeker (Farmville, Virginia, 1961), pp. 119-142. Reprinted by Julius Lawrence Rothman, ed., in The Cabellian: A Journal of the Second American Renaissance, III, No. 2 (Spring, 1971), 50-63.

IV.   CABELL'S TRANSLATION OF VIRGINIA   57

      Published in The Cabellian, II, No. 1 (Autumn, 1969), 1-11.

V.   A CASE OF LITERARY PIRACY?   77

      Presented as a paper before an American Literature section at the South Atlantic Modern Language Association, Miami Beach, 1962. Published in The Cabellian, I, No. 2 (Spring, 1969), 58-63.

VI. CABELL'S COMIC MASK   88

    Presented as a paper at the Cabell Seminar of
the Modern Language Association, New York, 1970. Published in The Cabellian, IV, No. 1 (Autumn, 1971), 1-8.

JAMES BRANCH CABELL AND SOUTHERN ROMANTICISM

In order to understand the extent to which James Branch Cabell was both influenced and repelled by Southern Romanticism, it is necessary, at the outset, to define the temper and direction of this movement in its relationship to that occurring simultaneously in the world at large.

The word Romanticism has several implications, according to A. O. Lovejoy in his book entitled <u>Essays in the History of Ideas</u>.[1] It may, on the one hand, indicate a return to nature and to primitivism, as was the case with such English poets as Joseph Warton, Wordsworth, Keats, and Shelley. On the other hand, it may concern itself with the faraway and the long ago. The German Goethe and the American Edgar Allan Poe were both fascinated by such romantic manifestations as the luxuriance of Gothic architecture, the mystery of early Celtic tales, or the horrors of the Inquisition. French Romanticists, such as Rousseau and Alfred de Musset, were chiefly preoccupied with exploring the terrain of a still more hidden and secret universe--that of the inner soul of man. Goethe and Novalis concentrated on one particular aspect of man's inner nature, the struggle of the individual to attain the unattainable, and thereby to make of himself a kind of minor deity in the everyday world.

The common denominator in all of these various manifestations of Romanticism was the exploration of the <u>remote</u> in time or in space. The Romanticist was from his genesis a world traveler, or a <u>mundivagant</u>, as Cabell would have said. He was wont <u>to journey</u> either far back or far forward in time; he traveled great distances horizontally upon the surface of the earth or vertically between Heaven and Hell; or he sought to dig to the very roots of nature, human or otherwise, to uncover the secrets of hidden, barely accessible universes.

The Southern Romanticist, however, adopted only two aspects of the romantic complex of ideas. In a sense, he was willing to travel vertically in space, as is manifested by his general acceptance of the Christian Heaven and Hell. He did not, however, seek in the skies above the Platonic ideal of the philosophers. Secondly, he traveled back in time--first, to the

Middle Ages and, later, to the eighteenth century.
From the Middle Ages, according to Cabell, he gleaned
three concepts: his conviction that he was God's
vicar upon earth, whose duty it was to right the
wrongs that exist; his belief that he must defend his
own honor at all costs; and his concept of domnei, or
woman worship, which with Cabell, as with poets from
the time of Homer, carried with it the implication of
the pursuit of the ideal, incarnated in the body of a
beautiful woman.[2]

The chivalric aspect of Southern Romanticism provided the richest nourishment to the genius of the younger James Branch Cabell. The tendency of the Southerner to see himself as a knight in shining armor riding forth to fight for a cause which he believed to be right provided Cabell's multi-volumed "Biography of the Life of Manuel" with many a crusader, who is set upon doing what he believes to be his duty, at no matter what expense to himself, or to anyone else either, as the older Cabell added ironically in a later volume.[3] The chivalric thread in Southern Romanticism enabled Cabell to create, also, his never-never land of Poictesme, that region so much like Virginia and yet so different from it, wherein the artist might move at will and breathe freely without fear of recrimination from his readers.

Later, instead of returning to the Age of Chivalry, the Southern mind preferred, after the events of the mid-nineteenth century, to go back only so far as its own Golden Age, the eighteenth century, the Age of Classicism, that age when men assumed the gallant attitude toward life which enabled them, as Cabell wrote, "to accept the pleasures of life leisurely and its inconveniences with a shrug."[4] Paradoxically, then, for romantic reasons, the South adopted in its daily life the tastes and standards of Neoclassicism.

This reversion to the more immediate past, coinciding, as it did, with Victorianism, led the aristocratic Southerner to place renewed emphasis, at least outwardly, upon measure and good taste, both in décor and in conduct. In spite of a thin film of Gothic architecture, which spread over the face of the South at the turn of the century, the Southerner continued to cherish the white columns of Monticello and the University of Virginia. The South still preferred the forthrightness and simple dignity of the great, four-square rooms of its colonial mansions along the James to the erratic little nooks and eccentric crannies of Gothic interiors. In behavior, as in architecture, the South continued to insist upon restraint and outward conformity in human relationships. Erratic behavior it deemed "tacky." Conversation, it felt, should not lead to altercation and to romantic turbulence. The Southerner, therefore, had to carefully restrict his words to small talk--to comments upon the weather and to inquiries as to health, for these were matters about which no one was apt to become greatly disturbed. The Southerner sedulously avoided controversial and personal matters, thereby rendering taboo the exploration of the inner recesses of the individual--of that area which the French romantics termed succinctly the moi. The Southerner consistently refused to embrace this personal aspect of Romanticism. Nor did he have much sympathy with the type of "itchy-footed" romantic who hankered after distant corners of the earth. The average Southerner was quite content to remain under his own blue skies, surrounded by his own warm friends. He wished to maintain the even tenor of his own life in his own milieu.

This classical frame of mind, which insisted upon restraint and decorum rather than a restless Bohemianism, produced in the South a life which possessed much beauty, harmony, and proportion. The South long seemed to the Southerner and to many a crass invading Northman to be the last outpost of charm and security in a world covered by the smoke of nineteenth- and twentieth-century industrialism. The Southerners maintained for themselves even in the face of tragedy a satisfactory and a satisfying manner of living, which had enormous appeal to the majority. They made of life itself an art.

This second reversion to the past, to the ideas of Neoclassicism, contributed likewise to the genius of Cabell. First, on the negative side, it furnished him with the impetus to rebel violently against the ways of the South which attempted to confine in a strait jacket the nonconforming artistic temperament. On the positive side, it provided him with the inspiration for his tales contained in the book specifically entitled Gallantry, which dealt with life in the seventeenth and eighteenth centuries. It also gave a modus vivendi to many of his middle-aged characters, in his books other than Gallantry, and to his younger protagonists when they had lost their chivalric illusions; for the chivalric attitude was, in the main, that of youth--of a young man or of a young nation--whereas the gallant attitude was that of the coming of age of an individual or of a people.

There was, in addition, a third attitude toward life, isolated and labeled by Cabell, an attitude which Cabell felt was peculiar to romantic artists, among whom he invariably classified himself. This attitude, termed by Cabell the _poetic_ attitude, causes the artist, who rebels against the imperfections and the unnecessary strictures of the world about him, to create from the raw material of everyday life a far better world than that which he has ever known.[5] If Cabell's criterion is applied to the South, the South, in its turn, shared with the romantic artist the poetic attitude, for the Southerner likewise attempted to create in his own mind a far more beautiful world than that which surrounded him. The South, then, by virtue of its very chivalry and its gallantry, was itself poetic.

Although Cabell and the South were alike in that they had both adopted the chivalric and gallant attitudes to some extent and that they had both desired to create the worlds they wanted from the raw materials of the life about them, yet they differed so significantly that their respective outlooks seemed, at first glance, to have little in common. In the first place, they were unlike in that they worked in different media. The South worked in life; Cabell worked in words. They differed, too, in that the chivalric South would not admit that it might be wrong, whereas Cabell always considered all human beliefs, including his own, suspect and something of a luxury. He thought that

> . . . human ideas are probably not ever correct about anything. It is certain we have no way of checking off the correctness of any human ideas. All human ideas . . . should be valued only as the playthings with which one purchases diversion. One plays with them during the night season of a not yet ended Walburga's Eve, upon which almost anything is rather more than likely to happen.[6]

Lastly, they differed in the types of Romanticism which they elected to make their own. The conservative agrarian South was willing to travel back in time only to the Ages of Chivalry and of Gallantry; in space it journeyed only to the Christian Heaven and Hell. In contrast, Cabell's mind ranged through all of time and all of space--through all myths and all history. In this process he became a mental vagabond upon the surface of the earth, a François Villon, who was bound to differ violently from his more provincial neighbors. He came to look upon himself as a Wandering Jew among men, one who had lived through the ages. In fact, time and time again in his romances, taking a cue from this favorite myth of his, he referred to himself as a Peripatetic Episcopalian. He was a modern-day Faust, who was content with no pat explanation of the universe. To this wanderer through all of time and all of space, the temporal, the finite, the particular took on a cosmic insignificance in the total scheme of affairs. The insistence of his neighbors upon their fixed little notions of life seemed ludicrous to this rebellious cosmopolite in a world "where almost anything is rather more than likely to happen."

Cabell's immense erudition and his sophistication had the effect of alienating him from his associates. When he detected what he considered to be flaws in the point of view of his neighbors, he could not refrain from telling them so. They, in their turn, naturally looked askance at the individual who disturbed their equanimity and came to resent bitterly his criticism. In Faust Goethe expressed skillfully the tension which has always existed between society and its critics when he wrote: "Die wenigen die was davon erkannt, . . . hat man von je gekreuzigt und verbrannt."[7]

As Cabell grew older and suffered the inevitable disillusionments of maturity, among which might be reckoned the shattering condemnation of Jurgen in the 1920's, he perfected a technique which had been practiced widely by such eighteenth-century critics of society as Montesquieu, the author of the Lettres Persanes. He developed more and more their habit of looking at himself and at his own people with the cold, impersonal eyes of a traveler from a far country. As a result of his observations, this stranger from Parnassus grew ever more rebellious against the fixed mores of his fellow Southerners, and he came to feel that the Southern chivalric attitude toward life, involving as it did a strictly fundamentalist religious position, created in the minds of the individuals who subscribed to it a deplorable priggishness and intolerance. He complained bitterly of these traits as he saw them manifested in his own people. *In Let Me Lie* (1947) he wrote of the average Virginian: "No power can shake his belief in his own eternal rightness," and likewise "no power in nature can upset the faith of a Virginian of the old school as to the myths among which he was reared, and of which he needs to be worthy."[8] His irritation at Virginians' implicit belief in what he considered to be their false illusions was even more clearly set forth in *Special Delivery*, when he wrote:

> Of beauty and of chivalry and of gray legions
> they spoke, and of a fallen civilization
> such as the world will not ever see again,
> and, for that matter, never did see; of a first
> permanent settlement, and of a Mother of
> Presidents, and of a republic's cradle, and
> of Stars and Bars, and of yet many other
> bygones, long ago at one with dead Troy and
> Atlantis. . . .[9]

In this passage Cabell undoubtedly had in mind the fact that Virginians insisted upon the truth of the Pocahontas story, even after historians had rejected most of the details surrounding it; that they believed in the first-white-settlement-in-America legend, in spite of the indisputable fact that Saint Augustine had been founded some forty-two years before Jamestown; and that they claimed Virginia Dare, the so-called "first" white child born in America, as their own, when actually some eight or ten boys--the Spaniards did not bother to count the girls--had been born in Florida, before Virginia Dare had been born in Virginia, actually on Roanoke Island, which is now not part of Virginia anyway, but of North Carolina.[10]

Cabell felt, too, that there was no hope that Virginia would ever abandon its myths, for, he complained, "Virginia did not read." Since it did not "honor any writer," no one felt inspired to write. "There were [therefore] no written words to outlive . . . the babblings" of their "demagogues," who spoke only "big words . . . in . . . praise [of Virginia], and in the praise of all her customs." Imitating Jeremiah, Cabell wrote, partly in resentment of the neglect accorded to his own words, "With all these never-idle talkers Virginia had played the wanton in a little corner, in the plashed mire of her stagnant backwaters, saying, Speak to me of my pre-eminence! And all they had spoken to the desire of Virginia, very egregiously."[11]

Because Cabell critized the South, he must not, however, be thought hostile to it. He loved his country, his state, his city, and his family, but he saw their shortcomings. Like Dante, who had bitterly reproached the city of Florence, which he loved above all other places on the face of the earth, so Cabell chastised Richmond, Virginia, and the South. On the other hand, Cabell himself would no doubt have been the first to spring to the defense of his homeland, had any stranger maligned it. And always it must be remembered that, regardless of what Cabell said about the South in his attempts to improve it, he always elected to live his life in Virginia, for he felt, along with his fellow Southerners, that he was far better off at home than he would have been anywhere else, and he wrote frequently with the deepest affection of Virginia--especially of the Northern Neck, which he seemed to consider a last haven of refuge, a Garden of Eden, in a world gone mad.

If Cabell had limited himself only to a carping criticism of the ways of the South, he and his work would have amounted to nothing. But this was not the case. From Cabell's rebellion against the world about him were born his speculations as to the springs of all human behavior. The best and most complete expression of his conclusions is contained in his "Biography of the Life of Manuel," that long allegory of the struggles of the human race from the thirteenth-century redeemer who had pulled himself up from the mire by his own bootstraps to the Virginians of Cabell's own lifetime.

Because of Cabell's dismay at the average Southerner's unwillingness to face what Cabell deemed to be the truth, and perhaps because of a similar inability which he must, at times, have detected in himself, he studied the phenomenon of human illusions in general. From this he came to the realization that mankind as a whole is loath to face reality. Man, it seems, must live by his dreams. He will not and cannot accept things as they are. Man dreams either of the past, when he believes that life has been better, or of the future, when he hopes that it will be better. If he dreams of the past, he takes refuge in ancestor worship and joins the D.A.R., the U.D.C., and the Association for the Preservation of Virginia Antiquities. If he dreams of the future, he envisages some hereafter of shimmering light and rainbow colors, wherein Grandfather Satan

will punish the sins of the wicked. If the dreamer is
really striving for justice, he believes that the sins
of the dreamer himself will be punished as well.
Because of his pride, then, he must, perforce, dream
of a hell in which the flames will be very high and
very hot indeed to punish adequately his own beautiful
crimes. Out of the cocoon of his own cranium man
spins the beautiful fabric of his own dreams. He
creates what he thinks "ought to be" rather than "what
is."

And why is it that people from time immemorial
have refused to face the truth? Cabell attributed
this human propensity, which is probably due in reality
to man's fears and to his insecurity, to man's dullness
and his vanity. Man's dullness will not permit him to
understand that he is simply a little midge[12] clinging
to the surface of a vast sphere, which is whirling
madly through space. Consequently, his vanity makes
him insist that he, as an individual, should be accorded
special attention by someone--if not by his immediate
associates in this life,[13] at least by a deity in the
life to come.

And life to most human beings, Cabell included, is,
at times, eminently unsatisfactory. The routine of life
itself, divested of its niceties--its candles, its lace
tablecloths, its silver tea sets--is ghastly. Birth
is bloody and cruel; death is corruption. The human
being in his progress through life is hideously and
irremediably alone. Even a man's own mate fails completely to understand his dreams, ambitions, and ideals.
A man's wife will not read his books but chatters fatu-
ously about the amount of money the books would bring
in were he to make certain changes in them. A man
and his wife talk at each other rather than with each
other. If there is often no real understanding between
a man and his wife, there is infinitely less between
man and the rest of the world.

Cabell presented a pathetic little picture of man's
utter incomprehensibility to his fellows in the
Harrowby-Kennaston episode near the close of The Cream
of the Jest. There Cabell brought together two men,
Dick Harrowby and Felix Kennaston, who, in many ways,
have much in common. Both are Richmonders who have
inherited sizable fortunes; both travel in the same social
circles; both have dabbled much in the occult. On one
occasion, for one brief golden moment, Dick Harrowby
finds that his callers, the Kennastons, and his own wife

seem miraculously disposed to listen briefly to his
talk of his hobby, that exploration of the hidden,
the occult, which had much in common with Felix
Kennaston's own interests. Yet Harrowby's pleasure
at being accorded a moment's attention is short lived,
for it is quenched first by Kennaston's rather flippant
treatment of Harrowby's subject and then by Mrs.
Harrowby's remark to the effect that if they allowed
Dick to start on his hobbies, he would bore them all to
death. She proposes, as women are wont to do, that they
all have a drink.

Harrowby's frustration at the interruption is indicated by his eagerness to resume the subject, which is absorbing to him, at least, and should have been to Kennaston, and his bitter disappointment when Cabell wrote laconically at Harrowby's thoughts: "And we obeyed her, and--somehow--got to talking of the recent thunderstorms, and getting in our hay, and kindred topics." This lack of anything remotely resembling comprehension and sympathy among human beings is emphasized when Cabell has Mrs. Harrowby, as soon as the Kennastons have left, remark cattily about the guests to whom she has just been so cordial that she wonders "how Mrs. Kennaston could keep on rouging and powdering at her age, and why Kennaston never had anything in particular to say for himself. 'Do you suppose it is because he has a swelled head over his little old book, or is he just naturally stupid?'"[14] she asks, with the Philistine's uneasy distrust of the aesthetic intelligence.

There are these four people, probably as well qualified as any in the world to understand each other. Their interests and environment are almost identical. For a brief moment there may have been some point of contact established among them, and yet all four float past each other and fail to communicate anything whatsoever to each other. In Beyond Life Cabell stated still more clearly the incomprehensibility of man to man when he wrote, "For each of us is babbling in the night, and has no way to make his fellows understand just what he would be at. It may be there is some supernal audience which sees and hears with perfect comprehension. Yes, such of course may be the case. But, in that event, I shudder to think of how we must provoke and bore that audience. . . ."[15]

As a result of the desolation of this life, man seeks refuge in his dreams. In The Cream of the Jest Felix Kennaston, clutching his Sigel of Scoteia, junkets back and forth between Lichfield (Richmond) and Poictesme in search of the ideal. He leaves this terrestrial soil and his talking-scolding wife, who, nevertheless, would lay down her life for him, and goes off to that never-never land where all is as it should be, where, at last, are perfect justice and beauty. In Poictesme, he catches fitful glimpses of the ideal, the girl of his dreams, la belle Ettarre, but Cabell, like a true romanticist, whose dominant trait is rebelliousness, could not allow even his own dreams to remain undisturbed. Like Don Quixote, who destroyed at a blow the painfully contrived cardboard visor to his helmet, and like Heine, who bitterly burst romantic bubbles that he had created, so Cabell rebelled even against his own dreams. Suppose his dreams were to come true? Would he be content? Would man be satisfied with what he had, if he had what he wanted? The answer to that question Cabell provided in Jurgen.

In Jurgen the Romanticist is vouchsafed a prolonged residence in Poictesme. And what does he find there? His beautiful maidens are for the most part a dreadful disappointment to him. Dorothy la Désirée, just after her assertions of love for the young Jurgen, meets Heitman Michael, the man whom she eventually marries. Guinevere, the beautiful bride of King Arthur, whom people praise for her freshness and for her chastity, has neither one nor the other, as Jurgen has good reason to know from personal experience. Anaïtis, the Cabellian representation of the fertility goddess of the Ancients, is a little oppressive in her ardor--so much so, in fact, that Jurgen is quite relieved when he becomes a solar myth, descends to Hades for six months, and so rids himself of her attractive, but insistent, presence. In Hell Jurgen has the rather doubtful privilege of marrying one of the most attractive, but dangerous, of females, the vampire Florimel, who is vacationing in the nether regions. Although he admires her beauty, yet her sharp little white teeth do serve constantly to remind him of her vocation, and even with this seductive creature, life degenerates into its usual tedium. They visit the "in-laws" and spend evenings with the Asmodeuses, where the gentlemen talk politics, much to the boredom of pretty little Florimel.

Through all of Jurgen's journeyings through the various dream worlds, he can have and can be just what he wants. Because it suits his fancy, he becomes successively Jurgen, the Duke of Logreus; Prince Jurgen

of Cocaigne; King Jurgen of Eubonia; Jurgen, the Emperor
of Noumaria; Pope John the Twentieth; and finally, when,
as a solar myth, he is forced to ascend into Heaven, he
sits on the throne of God himself. But never is he completely satisfied, and even on the very throne of God
he feels a gnawing discontent, for always a shadow had
attended him, "a shadow that makes all things not quite
satisfactory, not wholly to be trusted, not to be met
with frankness."[16] Cabell presented the common plight
of man most effectively when he described Jurgen's com-
munion with his own soul, as he sat splendidly enthroned
in Heaven.

> "And what will you do now?" says Jurgen,
> aloud. "Oh, fretful little Jurgen, you that
> have complained because you had not your
> desire, you are omnipotent over Earth and
> all the affairs of men. What now is your
> desire?" And sitting thus terribly
> enthroned, the heart of Jurgen was as
> lead within him, and he felt old and very
> tired. "For I do not know. Oh, nothing
> can help me, for I do not know what thing
> it is that I desire! And this book and
> this sceptre and this throne avail me
> nothing at all, and nothing can ever avail
> me; for I am Jurgen who seeks he knows not
> what."[17]

As even Heaven itself fails then to satisfy this
fastidious visitor from Earth, Jurgen, the knight-errant,
shrugs his shoulders, thereby indicating his transition
from the chivalric to the gallant attitude towards life,
and asks one of the four archangels who are in attendance
upon him, "the quickest way out of Heaven," for he wishes
to return to the more congenial illusions of Earth.
Although he has admired and envied much that he has seen
in Heaven, he feels that he cannot really believe in
what he has seen. Certainly there is little satisfaction
to be derived from the vague, empty beauty of Heaven.
Instead, he is beset with a great longing for that com-
fortable, prosaic life of his on Earth, and so he returns
of his own volition to the everyday world and to his own
wife, Dame Lisa, who nags frightfully, but who, nevertheless, is a companion to whom he has become accustomed.
His residence in the lands beyond common sense has
stripped him of all his illusions. Heaven is no more

satisfactory than Earth. This ideal destination of man is scarcely worth the struggle of attaining it.

Jurgen's chivalric ideal of women, too, has vanished into thin air along with his dreams of Heaven. He who had once worshiped all women for their "sacred, sweet intimidating beauty" now begins to suspect that women, also are akin to their parents; and are no wiser, and no more subtle, and no more immaculate, than the father who begot them."[18]

Jurgen has then finished his quest of the ideal with faith in nothing, "not even in his own unavoidable deductions."[19] He feels like "a rudderless boat that goes from wave to wave."[20] He knows nothing and he has nothing, for "man possesses nothing certainly save a brief loan of his own body."[21] When Cabell demolished Jurgen's illusions, he destroyed symbolically at the same time the illusions of a trinity composed of the poet Cabell, of the South, and of the entire human race.

Along with Jurgen's scepticism concerning the traditional concepts of Heaven and Hell he has, however, a profound regret that he can not retain the simple, innocent faith of his childhood. Cabell might well be considered as presenting his own point of view when he has Jurgen regret that he cannot believe in Jurgen's grandmother's God.[22]

Cabell's religion, in fact, was much like that of the sceptics of the eighteenth century. It resembled closely the philosophy evolved by such writers as Toland, Diderot, and D'Holbach. Cabell was impelled by much the same urge as was Diderot, when the latter called out, "Elargissez Dieu. Voyez-le partout où il est, ou dites qu'il n'existe point."[23] Diderot came to feel that matter in motion, which is constantly forming new combinations, is God. Cabell had something of the same idea, although he used different terms to express his concept. His matter in motion is symbolized by a stupid, deathless Russian, one Koshchei, the demiurge, who creates things as they are, even Jurgen's grandmother's heaven. This demiurge in the human species becomes the spirit of romance, which leads man to reach ever toward the stars, to dream himself ever upward. The spirit of romance is thus the creative principle, which, on the physical plane, creates oncoming life. Viewed in this light, Cabell's so-called erotic imagery, which was greatly condemned by the twenties, has a legitimate place in his books, for the sexual impulse is but the demiurge working in man, who is ever creating, ever producing new life, which will, in turn, work to bring about a heaven on earth. On the spiritual plane, the demiurge is the artistic impulse in man, which enables him to create art--to bring into being something which had not existed before. Man, and especially the artist, becomes perhaps God through this creative activity, for Cabell held something of the idea that Goethe set forth in his little poem entitled "Prometheus": the artist because of his creativity rivals God. Man, in the cosmos of both Goethe and of Cabell, is perhaps his own Prometheus.

Manuel, the hero of Cabell's great "Biography," becomes, therefore, a most significant character, for he is the great progenitor of that race of human beings whom Cabell traced through many centuries and through many countries in order to show man's gradual evolution from the cave man. Yet, throughout time, Cabell himself admitted rather regretfully, Manuel and his descendants, Jurgen included, remain one and all "pretty much the same in most times and stations, and come by varying roads" to "pretty much the same end."[24] The name Manuel is suggestive, nevertheless, of what might be wishful thinking on the part of both Cabell and of humanity as a whole. Manuel is probably a compound of the English word man and the Latin-French diminutive el, meaning "little." Manuel thus becomes "little man." The connotation of this name is heightened by its relationship to the Hebrew word Emmanuel, meaning "God is with us." It seems quite obvious, therefore, that Cabell meant the name Manuel to suggest that God, or the creative principle, is indwelling in the body of man himself. While Manuel is primarily a man of action, yet even this father of Cabell's brain children has some faint glimmer of light, which does impel him to try to make something of himself. The real man of ideas is, however, Jurgen, who has deluded himself into believing that he has seen Manuel, the incarnation of the redeemer, ride off into the west on his great silver stallion, much as Lee had ridden off on Traveler. Jurgen, who has thus caught a vision of the ideal, becomes the prototype of the knightly crusader, the young adventurer, who eventually learns, however, to shrug his shoulders, when his illusions prove to be vain. He does not die like Don Quixote, but he elects simply to return to real life and to live on with his earthly ideals, which he bequeaths to his progeny.

Cabell's somewhat pessimistic view of the essential

nature of man is brilliantly stated in one masterly paragraph in the preface to <u>Straws and Prayer-Books</u>.

> Fundamentally [he wrote] my protagonist does not change in any one of my eighteen volumes; but remains, instead, under all temporal garbs and all surface stainings, very much the same blundering male ape, reft of his tail and grown rusty at climbing, forever aspiring and yet forever cautious, forever hungering for companionship and for comprehension and for sympathy, and yet, none the less, retaining forever inviolate that frigid, and pale, and hard, small core of selfishness which . . . was the heart of Manuel. . . . Yes: I am afraid that, at bottom, under every permissible human grace and large human gesture, and under each of my three human attitudes, that obscure slight heart-trouble has been perpetuated in every one of the descendants of Manuel as ineradicably as it yet endures in all the race of Adam.[25]

Since romance or faith is man's only hope of salvation, Koshchei and romance then become synonymous terms. Man, ostensibly the underdog, though actually the vehicle of romance, thus becomes in Cabell's cosmology the Cinderella of a vast cosmic fairy tale. And man's greatest literary creation on Earth, the Holy Bible, is, then, by extension, the greatest romance of all. It "is past doubt [says Cabell] the boldest and the most splendid example of pure romance contrived by human ingenuity."[26] It is one vast Cinderella story, which sets forth, after "the disregard and contumely accorded God . . . from the Genesis of humanity," his "ultimate very public triumph celebrated amid the unimaginable pomp and fanfare of the vision seen from Patmos."[27] Christianity, too, Cabell regarded as the Cinderella legend set forth in more impressive terms.[28] He believed that if the accounts recorded in the Bible "really happened--if one great Author did in point of fact shape the tale thus, employing men and women in the place of printed words,--it very overwhelmingly proves that our world is swayed by a romancer of incalculable skill and imagination."[29]

And so to show his "confidence in this Author's literary abilities," Cabell, in The Cream of the Jest, has his protagonist, Felix Kennaston, be confirmed at his little neighborhood church, "to the delight of his wife and the approbation of his neighbors." Furthermore, Cabell reports that his hero is undeniably "pleased and flattered" when not long afterward he is elected to the vestry of the church to replace one "William T. Vartrey (of the Lichfield Iron Works)" who had not long before been "gathered to his grandfathers."[30]

Felix Kennaston therefore joins the Episcopal church to honor the Author of the Universe and at the same time to pay homage to Mother Sereda, the high priestess of conformity. Like Job, Kennaston seems to have been silenced by powerful arguments as to the greatness and glory of God.

In Beyond Life Cabell confirmed the suspicion that Kennaston had joined the church primarily to be doing what was expected of him rather than from any strong religious conviction, when the author borrowed the eighteenth-century technique of looking upon a human convention--a church service--with the puzzled, dispassionate eyes of a visitor from another planet.[31]

To Cabell a sane view of religion is rather the recognition of the Spirit of Romance as the First Cause and a veneration for this creative drive. Although later in his life, in Special Delivery, he did give evidence of feeling a need for a more personal God,[32] through most of his writings his godhead was something much akin to the Spirit of Affirmation of Goethe and to the Everlasting Yea of Carlyle. Nevertheless, he usually referred to the creative principle as the Author of the Universe, but to his Author of the Universe he refused to attribute omnipotence, for he felt that this world is much too imperfect to be the creation of an all-powerful deity. John Charteris in Beyond Life expresses Cabell's conception of the creative principle at work in man and in nature in these lines:

> . . . I prefer to take it that we are components of an unfinished world, and that we are but as seething atoms which ferment toward its making, if merely because man as he now exists can hardly be the finished product of any Creator whom one could very heartily revere. We are being made into something quite unpredictable, I imagine: and we are sustained, through the

purging and the smelting, by an instinctive
knowledge that we are being made into something better. For this we know, quite incom-
municably, and yet as surely as we know that
we will to have it thus.
    And it is this will that stirs in us to
have the creatures of earth and the affairs
of earth, not as they are, but "as they
ought to be," which we call romance. But
when we note how visibly it sways all life
we perceive that we are talking about God.33

    If the South has its dreams and its illusions, it is not unique in this respect, for it shares this character- istic with the whole human race. Man must have his dreams in order to exist at all. Even though man's dreams may have no basis whatsoever in reality, yet through striving to fulfill his wishes man creates what he wants. Because he does not want what he then has, he ever dreams himself upward, and so he himself becomes Goethe's "living stair- way," which leads him to Heaven.

    The chivalry and the gallantry of the South thus pro- vided Cabell with the raw materials for his poesy. Although Cabell had drunk deep of such continental authors as Goethe and the French and English rationalists, yet Southern Romanticism furnished him with the initial dynam- ics governing his philosophy of life and of art. To the South, Cabell owed a great debt of gratitude; and, needless to say, the South, in its turn, and Virginia, in particu- lar, should not forget to pay homage to this great stylist, for, whatever his faults may be, there is no writing quite like his in twentieth-century America.

NOTES

[1] A.O. Lovejoy, Essays in the History of Ideas (Baltimore: The Johns Hopkins University Press, 1948), pp. 228-253.

[2] James Branch Cabell, Chivalry: Dizain des Reines, The Works of James Branch Cabell, Storisende Edition (New York: Robert M. McBride & Company, 18 vols., 1927-1930), V, 4-5. (Unless otherwise stated, all other references to Cabell's works in this book are to the various volumes in the Storisende Edition.)

[3] Cabell, Let Me Lie: Being in the Main an Ethnological Account of the Remarkable Commonwealth of Virginia and the Making of Its History (New York: Farrar, Straus and Company, 1947), p. 285.

[4] Cabell, The Cords of Vanity: A Comedy of Shirking, Works, XII, ix.

[5] Cabell, Beyond Life: Dizain des Démiurges, Works, I, ix-x.

[6] Ibid., p. x.

[7] Johann Wolfgang von Goethe, Faust, Commentiert von Erich Trunz (Hamburg: Christian Wegner Verlag, 1963), p. 26.

[8] Cabell, Let Me Lie, pp. 284-285.

[9] [James] Branch Cabell, Special Delivery: A Packet of Replies (New York: Robert M. McBride & Company, 1933), p. 52. (After the completion of the Storisende Edition in 1930, Cabell published his subsequent books under the name of Branch Cabell until There Were Two Pirates in 1946.)

[10] Cabell, Let Me Lie, pp. 45-76.

[11] Cabell, Special Delivery, pp. 51-53.

[12] Cabell, Beyond Life, Works, I, 261-262.

[13] Ibid., p. 260.

[14] Cabell, The Cream of the Jest [and] The Lineage of Lichfield: Two Comedies of Evasion, Works, XVI, 206-207.

[15] Cabell, Beyond Life, Works, I, 259-260.

[16] Cabell, Jurgen: A Comedy of Justice, Works, VI, 319.

[17] Ibid., pp. 306-307.

[18] Ibid., pp. 338-339.

[19] Ibid., p. 340.

[20] Ibid., p. 341.

[21] Ibid., p. 342.

[22] Ibid., p. 305.

[23] J. Assézat et Maurice Tourneux, eds., Pensées philosophiques, Oeuvres complètes de Diderot (Paris: Garnier Frères, 1876). I, 138.

[24] Cabell, The Lineage of Lichfield, Works, XVI, 251-252,

[25] Cabell, Straws and Prayer-Books: Dizain des Diversions, Works, XVII, xviii.

[26] Cabell, Beyond Life, Works, I, 122.

[27] Ibid., p. 120.

[28] Ibid.

[29] Ibid., p. 122.

[30] Cabell, The Cream of the Jest, Works, XVI, 157.

[31] Cabell, Beyond Life, Works, I, 173-174.

[32] Cabell, Special Delivery, p. 234.

[33] Cabell, Beyond Life, Works, I, 270.

JAMES BRANCH CABELL: A LATTER-DAY ENLIGHTENER

Americans have been puzzled by Cabell's theology. To American Fundamentalists and to good British Anglicans Cabell's views on religion seem ambiguous, to say the least. An Englishman, Desmond Tarrant, apparently wanted the subject of his critical biography, <u>James Branch Cabell: The Dream and the Reality</u>, to wear a mantle of Christian respectability. He wrote that Cabell had a positive and indeed a Christian belief.[1] He based his remark on Cabell's conclusion in <u>Beyond Life</u> that God is the spirit of romance in man--that is, the desire to have "the creatures of earth and the affairs of earth, not as they are, but 'as they ought to be'"[2] Although, on the surface, Cabell's words may be interpreted as being quite orthodox, yet, actually, throughout most of his writing Cabell came close to Voltaire's position that, if there were no God, humankind would have had to invent him. Cabell felt, on the whole, that religion is something of a luxury which man gives himself to enable him to endure the harsh realities of life and of death.

A detailed study of Cabell and of the eighteenth-century Enlighteners confirms the fact that Cabell was writing, much of the time, in their tradition. Enlighteners, as a type, were usually impatient with religious conformists because of their intolerance--that trait labeled by Voltaire <u>l'infâme</u>. They were irritated, too, by the lack of correspondence between Christian beliefs and Christian ethics. The Inquisition was still raging in eighteenth-century France, where people well into the century were being imprisoned, exiled, and tortured for their failure to conform to the dogma of the Catholic church. While Cabell was not confronted with a situation which was so cruel and inhuman as that in Europe, yet he, too, was constantly being annoyed by the Fundamentalism of the Bible belt in the South, which he felt was scarcely consonant with the questionable ethics of his fellow-Southerners. Occasionally, he touched upon the real canker in the hearts of all white Southerners--their treatment of the Negroes. For instance, in a chapter in <u>The Rivet in Grandfather's Neck</u>, called "Virginia Quite Understands," Cabell speculated briefly on what the family maid, a mulatto named Virginia, might really be thinking behind her "pleasant yellow face as imperturbable as an idol's."[3] Although Cabell, like most other white Southerners, rarely touched upon the subject of the exploitation of the Negroes, yet throughout his books there is the implication, which sometimes becomes most explicit, that all is not as well as it should be in this Eldorado, which is Virginia.

Because of their disillusionment with mankind, the Enlighteners, especially in France, used, for the most part, ridicule, rather than downright denunciation, to attack their adversaries. They had learned that raillery is an effective means of correcting opinion from one of the most influential of the English Enlighteners, the third Earl of Shaftesbury, whose collected essays, published early in the eighteenth century under the title <u>The Characteristics of Men, Manners, Opinions, Times, etc.</u>, were highly esteemed by the French. Although Cabell never mentioned Shaftesbury by name throughout his work, yet he might have imbibed his techniques and ideas indirectly from Shaftesbury's French followers and from Pope, whose <u>Essay on Man</u>, based supposedly on Bolingbroke's notes from Shaftesbury's essays, gave Cabell the title, <u>Straws and Prayer-Books</u>,[4] for one of the volumes of his "Biography." It is altogether possible, too, that Cabell might have had direct contact with Shaftesbury's essays in a course devoted to logic, ethics, and the history of philosophy, which he took his senior year at William and Mary.[5] Since Shaftesbury is generally considered one of the most significant of the moral philosophers of the eighteenth century, Cabell might have read all or parts of the <u>Characteristics</u> in his undergraduate days, for, at times, his techniques and, occasionally, his actual words resemble rather closely those of the Englishman. Of course, this similarity may also be due to the fact that people of like mind frequently express themselves in a similar fashion.

At any rate, Shaftesbury, the eighteenth-century Enlighteners, and Cabell all used similar literary techniques--irony, exaggeration, understatement, and the eye of innocence--to combat what they deemed to be the four main facets of orthodox religion: first, the belief in an anthropomorphic deity; second, the esteem accorded to the sacred writings which perpetuate this belief; third, the credence in the miracles which strengthen and enforce the belief; and, fourth, the resultant activities--both the rituals and the everyday behavior--by which devotees express their belief.

The first target of attack of the great sceptics of history has usually been the nature of the deities whom the masses revere. Cabell, like the eighteenth-century Enlighteners and others of their ilk, was generally of the opinion that the finite brain of man is utterly incapable of comprehending the Infinite. The deists, the most orthodox of the liberals of the late seventeenth and eighteenth centuries, did entertain for a time a watered-down, common-denominator sort of god, whom they thought of first as a clockmaker and then as the Grand Architect of the Universe, but even he became, eventually, in the pages of the later Diderot and the Baron d'Holbach, only dynamic energy which takes on organization. Voltaire, again and again, attacked the belief in an anthropomorphic deity by exaggerating this conception to the point of absurdity. He liked to create in his tales, such as <u>Zadig</u>, an ironical situation in which a heavenly visitant appears to an earthling and, at the very moment of the great revelation, quixotically advises the poor mortal to cease troubling his head about esoteric matters, which he can never comprehend in any event, and to go about his earthly affairs, which are within his grasp.

Cabell adopted Voltaire's use of hyperbole in <u>Smirt</u>, the first volume of a trilogy labeled by Cabell "The Nightmare Has Triplets." Exaggerating the Southerners' implicit faith in a very human deity, he brought God, termed by Cabell the "All-Highest," face to face with a smart young whippersnapper named "Smirt." Smirt and the All-Highest chat cosily with each other, while reposing on billowy clouds. In this conversation, Cabell "out-Voltaired" Voltaire in his exaggeration, his understatement, and his irony by reversing the usual relationship between God and man. He elevated Smirt to the greatness of God, reduced God to the size of man, and made the King of Heaven deferential to Smirt, the earthling. After all, why should God not be respectful? Had it not been Smirt and his fellow human beings who had brought the creator of all things into being in the first place and had given him human form?

In the course of this astral conversation, Cabell managed also to cast aspersion upon the second target of the Enlighteners--the Holy Scriptures. Both the eighteenth-century Illuminati and their twentieth-century descendant accomplished their end by attacking, in actuality, the mind of humankind, who, they all felt, of course, was really responsible for God's "masterpiece"--the Bible. The human targets of the two periods differ, however. The eighteenth-century Enlighteners liked to vilify the <u>authors</u> of the so-called "word of God." They played up the <u>ignorance</u> and poverty of the Jews, who were represented by them as an obscure people dwelling at the far eastern end of the Mediterranean Sea. By this means, they hoped to reveal the irony of a situation which would allow great churches and governments to be founded upon the pronouncements of a people who were scarcely able to govern themselves, let alone half the world. The French seem to have taken their cue from a passage in Shaftesbury's "Soliloquy, or Advice

to an Author," in which the Englishman, early in the
eighteenth century, set forth a line of thought which subsequent Enlighteners were to adopt. In this work, in
1710, Shaftesbury had written:

> The simplicity of the people [the Jews] must
> certainly have been very great, when the best
> disciples had their heads so running upon
> their loaves, that they were apt to construe
> every divine saying in a belly sense. . . .
> No wonder if the better and nobler self was
> left as a mystery to a people who of all
> human kind were the most grossly selfish,
> crooked, and perverse.[6]

This line of attack was followed by Voltaire in a little
poem, written while he was still quite a young man, called
"Le Pour et le contre," in which he spoke of the Jews as
"un peuple obscur, imbécile, et volage."[7] Similarly,
d'Holbach, in his Christianisme dévoilé, marveled at the
fact that an obscure Jew could have managed to persuade
people that he was the Messiah and so played upon the
ignorance and abjectness of the disciples.[8]

In his attack upon human intelligence, Cabell did not
follow the lead of the English and French by singling out
the Jews, specifically. It was not the fashion to do so,
at least in print, in twentieth-century America, and Cabell
was too much of a cosmopolite to have done so in any case.
Instead, he found another scapegoat upon which to pin dullness and lack of understanding. He found exactly what he
needed, not in the authors of Holy Writ, but in the receivers,
his own compatriots--his beloved, but unperceptive Southern
neighbors--whom he deemed much too immature and perverse
to understand any but the most human type of God.

In Smirt, then, Cabell created an ironical situation in
which he has the All-Highest ask his visitor in a timid,
halting voice whether it might not be a good idea for the
heavenly writer to revise his book--the Holy Bible--to bring
it up to date, so that it might be more in line with modern
theology. Smirt shudders at such a proposal, for he feels,
much as a father would, that he must protect this creation
of his "from the cruel and silent derision" which he is
certain "the All-Highest would incur, quite inevitably, by
making any more revelations to mankind in the present state
of American letters."[9] Such a measure, he feels, would be
especially deplorable in the South, for the South, because
of its persistent anti-intellectualism, would remain

steadfastly "silent and unscornful, not heeding this book, or any other book."10

By this adroit combination of the exaggeration of human vanity and of the irony of a situation in which the finite mind of man believes that it can comprehend the Unknowable, both the eighteenth-century Enlighteners and Cabell managed to communicate to their readers their idea that man's concept of God is ever shifting and, hence, completely unreliable.

The third target of most Illuminati is human credence in miracles and oracles. Again, they usually resort to ridicule to set forth their conviction that too specific a belief in the Unknowable is impossible for humankind. To drive home their point, they frequently use women and children as prime examples of the credulous, for the more sophisticated members of society usually feel that women, children, and peasants are among the most simple-minded, if not the most foolish, of mankind. Fontenelle, in his Histoire des oracles, had an episode in which a gold tooth, which had "miraculously" appeared in the mouth of a child, was eventually revealed to be a hoax, for the tooth had been skillfully covered with gold foil. Likewise, in the Silver Stallion, one of the volumes of his "Biography," Cabell used a child as a point of departure to show that a whole religion may come into being as the result of a preposterous story concocted by a small boy, Jurgen, to protect himself from being punished for running away from home. He claimed that he had seen the transfiguration and assumption into heaven of Dom Manuel, the hero and progenitor of a large and important family. Eventually, his words were generally accepted as gospel truth by the members of his society.11 "Enlighteners," then, as a group, seem to enjoy concocting situations which reveal the fraudulence, ignorance, or, at best, the innocence of those who attach too much importance to earthly manifestations of the supernatural.

Cabell was especially scornful of the doctrine of the resurrection of the body so specifically insisted upon by the creed of his own Episcopal church. In his comment upon this subject, he resorted to indecencies reminiscent of those of Voltaire in La Pucelle. He subjected this doctrine, which is intoned unthinkingly Sunday after Sunday by hundreds of Christians all over the world, to the most scathing and indecorous satire, when he wrote on a situation which might possibly occur at the Last Judgment:

> . . . I am meditating, this afternoon, upon
> the sociology of Doomsday. The dead will
> arise . . . with their bowels, which will
> undoubtedly continue to function. In Our
> Father's house are many outhouses. Yes,
> there will be comfort stations in Para-
> dise with millions of rest rooms; and it
> is a solemn thought to reflect upon the
> holy persons enthroned in them every
> morning.[12]

Man is indeed naïf, thought Cabell, to insist upon the resurrection of the body in its physical form.

The fourth target of attack of these self-appointed critics of society is the outward manifestation of inner beliefs, both in the form of man's rituals, in which he honors his god, and in his everyday behavior, in which he honors or dishonors his fellowmen.

In order to show what they deem the meaninglessness of most religious observances, the liberal writers in any society frequently use a device which has long been a favorite with social critics; they subject human activity, especially its ceremonial observances, to the cold, objective eye of an outsider. This so-called "eye of innocence" is effective because it reduces the people observed to the status of addlepates, while the onlooker takes on the lofty superiority of a visitor from Olympus.

Shaftesbury, in his "Miscellaneous Reflections," used this means to criticize the doctrine of apostolic succession. He imported an Indian to England, had him taken to several churches, and let him observe Anglican services, until the Indian asked "who those persons were whom he observed haranguing so long with such authority from a high place." He was told that "they were ambassadors from the Almighty."[13] With his Indian background he assumed, then, that they must be ambassadors from the sun. Later, the confusion and the lack of understanding of the young Indian was shown when he hazarded the guess that the preachers in dissenting churches must be ambassadors from the moon.[14] Perhaps the best known and the most complete example of the use of this device was provided by the Lettres persanes of Montesquieu, who imported two Persians, à la Shaftesbury, into France and had them reveal through their wonderment and their subsequent comments the weaknesses in French society.

Cabell, then, writing in a time-honored tradition, used the "eye of innocence" to reveal his own views on what appeared to him to be the meaninglessness of most religious observances and the puzzling behavior of the clergy. He, too, wrote in the same vein as had Shaftesbury concerning religious observances.

> I must set about this by putting on my best raiment,--for, again like children, we need must "dress up" for everything we "play at,"-- and by going into a building of which the roof is indecorously adorned with a tall phallic symbol. . . . There, too, we perform a drill, of standing, sitting and kneeling, and we read and sing archaic observations from little books. . . . An honest gentleman, whose conduct upon week-days I cordially revere, emerges from the vestry, . . . and devotes some twenty minutes to revising one or another well-meant utterance of Christ into conformity with more modern ideas. The plates are passed, into which we put money, to pay for the heating, lighting and general upkeep of the building, and the living expenses of the clergyman and the janitor. Now all this is likewise more or less harmless, yet, when sanely viewed, it is difficult to connect in any way with religion.[15]

Much of what Christians do and have done Cabell and his kind have found infinitely difficult to connect in any way with religion. They find men, in general, too simple-minded, weak, and inefficient to put their theories into practice in their daily lives. Just as had his eighteenth-century predecessors, Cabell found the rapacity and cruelty of professed Christians in the New World one of the most difficult manifestations of religion to comprehend. Furthermore, in Cabell's case, his disapproval of the Spaniards' mistreatment of the Indians might have been a means of attacking obliquely whole groups of people who victimize other, more helpless nations or races in the name of religion. In his book, The First Gentleman of America, Cabell adopted, then, an attitude similar to that set forth by Voltaire in his play Alzire, in which the Frenchman had complained bitterly of the cupidity of los padres in Paraguay. By an adroit combination of hyperbole and understatement, the Virginian made clear his position on the matter of the exploitation of one people by another who profess to be Christians when he wrote:

> . . . all stalwart Spain delighted to hear about the . . . unstinted gold which a fair marksman could get in the west, so very easily, without

any awkward twinges of conscience, by shooting down like partridges a few hundred unarmed infidels. So, in most cases, it was gold of which the brave adventurers, who went to America dreamed. It was gold for which they sought, and gold which they demanded from the Indians, and gold which they got hourly, by one means or another, now that the heathen west had begun to allure all hardy Christians who hungered for wealth or who loved adventure, or who needed to escape from the unwelcome attentiveness of the police.[16]

Although most of the champions of free thought have deplored the bloody trail which Christianity has streaked through the centuries, yet, many of them were, in their daily lives, only closet heroes. For this reason, they all indulged, at times, in a species of seeming duplicity, by which they were, evidently, attempting to protect themselves from the shafts of their adversaries, or perhaps, in some moods, they really were sincere, for man's mind is ever inconsistent and vacillating. Most of the eighteenth-century Enlighteners performed, at intervals, the rituals of their respective religions. Moreover, they had the habit of imbedding in their work curious confessions of faith, which do not always seem to be in harmony with their usual patterns of thought. These confessions are strikingly similar both in content and in tone. They all call attention to their writers' professed orthodoxy, while, at the same time, they suggest the inability of the persons who had composed them to understand the Christian mysteries. Most of these passages manage to convey an impression of irony, however, partly because of the words themselves and partly because of the overall purpose of the works in which they occur.

Shaftesbury inserted his "confession" into one of the most liberal of his essays, the "Miscellaneous Reflections," in which he had written:

> . . . we can with confidence declare that we have never in any writing, public or private, . . . acquitted ourselves otherwise than as just conformists to the lawful church; so we may, in a proper sense, be said faithfully and dutifully to embrace these holy mysteries, even in the minutest particulars, and without the least exception on account of their amazing depth.[17]

Since this is followed by a descant on the accidents which have befallen Holy Writ, it becomes obvious that Shaftesbury did not put much stock in the infallibility of the Sacred Word.

Diderot, too, in his Pensees philosophiques, the deists' rejoinder to the tormented Pascal, professed his allegiance to a religion which he found difficult to understand since he had no concrete knowledge upon which to base his beliefs. He wrote:

> Je suis né dans l'église catholique, apostolique et romaine et je me soumets de toute ma force à ses décisions. Je veux mourir dans la religion de mes pères, et je la crois bonne autant qu'il est possible à quiconque n'a jamais eu aucun commerce immédiat avec la Divinité et qui n'a jamais été témoin d'un miracle. Voilà ma profession de foi; je suis presque sûr qu'ils seroient mécontent bien qu'il n'en ait peut-être pas un entre eux qui soit en état d'en faire une meilleure.[18]

Diderot, then, in his confession professed an allegiance to the religion into which he had been born and in which he hoped to die, even though he had never had any direct relationship with the Divinity nor had ever witnessed a miracle. He, thereby, paid lip service, at least, to beliefs for which he felt there were no adequate proofs.

Finally, we have Cabell's seemingly docile profession of faith, which contains the usual attestation concerning his performance of the requisite Christian ritual, accompanied with his bewilderment as to what it is he is worshiping. His remarks, too, are pervaded with the same note of irony as that found in the confessions of Shaftesbury and of Diderot.

> I need but tell you that I am a communicant of the Protestant Episcopal Church of America. I accept its creeds (both of them; and including of course the Thirty-Nine Articles) as being, in so far as I can understand their statements, quite possibly true. The remaining and the major portions of the tenets of my church I regard as indisputable, if but because they convey to me no earthly meaning, and nobody can dispute the incomprehensible. You cannot, for example, rationally deny that you believe in the Holy Ghost until somebody has

provided you with some faint notion of the Holy
Ghost. Pending that, I find no great difficulty
in accepting his existence, very much as I
accept the existence of the Amir of Afghanistan,
without forming any mental concept of either.[19]

At times, Cabell's attitude seemed to resemble that of
Rousseau, who, occasionally, came close to embracing orthodox Christianity, as he did, for example in his touching
and beautiful "Profession de foi du vicaire Savoyard,"
which Cabell must certainly have known, for students of
French literature are introduced to this beautiful passage
from Émile early in their careers. In this work devoted
to the education of a young man, Rousseau had written:

> Je vous avoue aussi que la sainteté de
> l'Évangile est un argument qui parle à mon
> coeur, et duquel j'aurois même regret de trouver
> quelque bonne résponse. . . . Voyez les livres
> des philosophes avec toute leur pompe: qu'ils
> sont petits près de celui-là! Se peut-il
> qu'un livre à la fois si sublime et si simple
> soit l'ouvrage des hommes? . . . Est-ce là
> le ton d'un enthousiaste ou d'un ambitieux
> sectaire? Quelle douceur, quelle pureté dans
> ses moeurs! quelle grace touchante dans ses
> instructions! . . . quelle profonde sagesse
> dans ses discours! quelle présence d'esprit, quelle
> finesse et quelle justice dans ses réponses! quel
> empire sur ses passions! Où est l'homme, où est
> le sage qui sait agir, souffrir et mourir sans
> foiblesse et sans ostentation? Quand Platon
> peint son juste imaginaire couvert de tout
> l'opprobre du crime, et digne de tous les prix
> de la vertu il peint trait pour trait Jésus-Christ.[20]

Much of the same tone--the desire to believe, coupled
with an inability to accept the Christian miracle--is present
in the words which Jurgen, one of Cabell's most significant
characters, addresses to his God.

> "God of my grandmother [says Jurgen], I can-
> not quite believe in You, and Your doings as they
> are recorded I find incoherent and a little droll.
> Yet I am glad the affair has been so arranged
> that You may always now be real to brave and
> gentle persons who have believed in and have wor-
> shiped and have loved You.

"God of my grandmother, I cannot quite believe in You, yet I am not as those who would come peering at you reasonably. I, Jurgen, see you only through a mist of tears. For You were loved by those whom I loved greatly a long while ago. . . . And it seems to me that dates and manuscripts and the opinions of learned persons are very trifling things beside what I remember, and what I envy!"[21]

Sometimes, as in Beyond Life, Cabell looked upon the Bible as a vast Cinderella tale and as the masterpiece of romance.[22] He felt that if the events in the Bible did really happen, they prove "that our world is swayed by a Romancer of incalculable skill and imagination."[23] This attitude would seem to lend support to the contention that Cabell had a positive belief in Christianity, were it not followed by book upon book in which Cabell poked fun at Holy Writ. For example, in one of his subsequent works, he called a saint whom he had created "Holmendis,"[24] obviously meaning to suggest by this name that the latter's function was to mend the holes in "Hol-e-y" Writ.

Fundamentally, the quarrel which most Enlighteners had with religion is with the pettiness of human conceptions and with the excesses of religious fanaticism. Perhaps Cabell's mistake, like that of most intellectuals, was in expecting the rank and file of mankind to think in abstract terms.

Cabell, then, did have much in common with the long line of Illuminati, who had their heyday in the eighteenth century, although this type of thinking has had its representatives throughout much of recorded time. Through most of his books, Cabell did write in a definite literary tradition--a tradition which was at its most explicit in the work of the eighteenth-century French Enlighteners.

While the sceptics, especially the self-appointed Enlighteners, in any society are frequently feared and disliked by the masses of men, yet they do perform a valuable function. By making men take a look at their own assumptions and behavior, they provide a valuable antidote against dogmatism and fanaticism, which can become dangerous if allowed to rage unrestrained or if it is misapplied. In the twentieth century, for example, many Fundamentalists in the South used the Bible to support their belief that segregation is the will of God. The agnostic serves to counteract the complacency which can lead to stagnation, inflexibility, and cruelty. On the other hand, religion, if wisely and sanely followed, can give

men the hope and charity which are sorely needed in all
stages of human history. Perhaps the best solution for
both groups, the believers and the sceptics, is to practice
the tolerance and forbearance which the great progenitor
of the Christian religion tried to instill into his followers during his own lifetime and which people have largely
ignored. The qualities which he preached would provide the
synthesis of the two extremes.

NOTES

[1] Desmond Tarrant, James Branch Cabell: The Dream and the Reality (Norman, Oklahoma: University of Oklahoma Press, 1967), pp. 76-77.

[2] Cabell, Beyond Life, Works, I, 270.

[3] Cabell, The Rivet in Grandfather's Neck: A Comedy of Limitations, Works, XIV, 58.

[4] Alexander Pope, An Essay on Man, Epistle II, ll. 275-276, 279-280.

[5] William Leigh Godshalk, "James Branch Cabell at William and Mary: The Education of a Novelist," The William and Mary Review, V, No. 2 (Spring, 1957), 5.

[6] Anthony, Earl of Shaftesbury, "Soliloquy, or Advice to an Author," Characteristics of Men, Manners, Times, etc., ed. John M. Robertson (London: Grant Richards, 1900), I, 184.

[7] Louis Moland, ed., "Le Pour et le contre, "Oeuvres complètes de Voltaire (Paris: Garnier Frères, 1879), IX, 470.

[8] Paul Thiry, Baron d'Holbach, Le Christianisme dévoilé, ou examen des principes et des effets de la religion chrétienne (Londres: [Nancy: Leclerc], 1767), p. 53.

[9] [James] Branch Cabell, Smirt: An Urban Nightmare (New York: Robert M. McBride & Co., 1934), p. 64.

[10] Ibid., p. 63.

[11] Cabell, The Silver Stallion: A Comedy of Redemption, Works, III, 3-5.

[12] Cabell, Smirt, p. 183.

[13] Shaftesbury, "Miscellaneous Reflections," Characteristics, II, 366.

[14] Ibid.

[15] Cabell, Beyond Life, Works, I, 173-174.

[16] [James] Branch Cabell, The First Gentleman of America: A Comedy of Conquest (New York: Farrar & Rinehart, Inc., 1942), pp. 14-15.

[17] Shaftesbury, "Miscellaneous Reflections," Characteristics, II, 352.

[18] Diderot, Pensées philosophiques, Oeuvres, I, 153.

[19] Cabell, Special Delivery, pp. 221-222.

[20]Armand-Aubrée, eds., *Émile, Oeuvres complètes de J.-J. Rousseau* (Paris, 1832), III, 459-461.

[21]Cabell, *Jurgen*, *Works*, VI, 304-305.

[22]Cabell, *Beyond Life*, *Works*, I, 120.

[23]*Ibid.*, 122.

[24]Cabell, *The Figures of Earth: A Comedy of Appearances*, *Works*, II, 271.

CABELL AND HIS CRITICS

James Branch Cabell, perhaps more than any other author who has ever lived, provided his readers with a vast amount of autobiographical material both in fictional and in essay form, with the intention, perhaps, of facilitating the writing of commentaries on his works, should his books outlive their author. For this reason, the work of Cabell provides the reader with ample material for making a case study of the effect of criticism upon a writer and of the means he may adopt to answer the sallies of his adversaries.

The relationship between a writer and his public, especially his immediate associates, has traditionally been strained and uneasy. Because the writer must spend long hours in his study, crossing, what seem to him, at least, to be ever-new frontiers of thought, he appears to the ordinary citizen to be growing ever more remote, vapourish, impractical, and down-gyved. On the other hand, the average man must appear to the writer to be an insensitive, stupid dolt, who makes little effort to understand the most elementary of the ideas brought back by the writer from Audela, as Cabell termed the world beyond common sense.

The problem of the artist in society is not a new one, by any means. Writers as diverse as Diderot, Goethe, Hawthorne, Mann, Kafka, Proust, and Joyce have dealt with the effort of the author to establish a satisfactory rapport with his public. The problem must have been an especially acute one, however, for James Branch Cabell. In Cabell we have the spectacle of a highly sophisticated and erudite intellect set down in what he considered a totally uncongenial atmosphere. This spiritual descendant of Heraclitus, Homer, Dante, Francois Villon, Rabelais, Voltaire, and Goethe was a human anachronism on the loose in what to him was Philistia.

Naturally, he was destined not to be understood by many of the people about him. He was hurt by the lack of attention that was paid to him by his Virginia neighbors, and he was resentful of what he considered the undiscerning criticism of professional critics outside of Virginia. Because of his hurt and resentment at the indifference of his own people and the hostility of outsiders, he developed what was almost a persecution complex and filled his later books with complaints directed against the human race, in general, and Virginians, in particular.

The questions that present themselves to the mind of the reader as he turns the pages of such books as <u>Smirt</u>, <u>Special Delivery</u>, and <u>Let Me Lie</u> are: How much was Cabell justified in his feeling that Virginia was neglecting him, what were the causes of the hostility which both outsiders and Virginians exhibited toward his books, and how did Cabell react to both groups?

Whatever Cabell must have felt concerning the injustice of the criticism of outsiders and the lack of attention of Virginians, he certainly should not have been too greatly disappointed by the <u>amount</u> of the attention, at least, which he received from the large newspapers and magazines with a national circulation.

Because Cabell represented a new force in American literature, something that was completely alien to the sentimentality and the Puritanism that had dominated letters in America from the Victorian era, he caught the public eye and was reviewed extensively, if not always favorably, both in this country and abroad. <u>The Cumulative Book Review Digest</u>, which came into existence in 1905, in time to record the notices of Cabell's second published volume, <u>The Line of Love</u>, lists in the fifty years from 1905 to 1955, the date of Cabell's last book, <u>As I Remember It</u>, a minimum of 264 reviews of Cabell's work appearing in major American and English newspapers and magazines. This number does not include, of course, innumerable reviews appearing in lesser publications all over the country.

In addition to the reviews of the Americans and of the English, there were a number of studies of Cabell by people of other nationalities. Some were merely book reviews of the traditional type; others were essays on his style or on his philosophy. There were at least nine French notices of his work, four German, three Australian, two Swedish, one South African, and one Italian. In addition, Cabell has been translated into a number of foreign languages, a tribute in itself.

Most of the significant histories of American literature from the banning of Jurgen in 1920 to the present contain sizeable sections devoted to the work of James Branch Cabell. These range in enthusiasm from Vernon Parrington's eulogy of Cabell entitled "The Incomparable Mr. Cabell" in his Main Currents of American Thought[1] in 1930 to Willard Thorp's much less commendatory remarks in his American Writing in the Twentieth Century,[2] published in 1960.

In addition, there have been several larger studies of Cabell--entire books (rather slim ones to be sure) or large sections of books. There were, for example, H. L. Mencken's James Branch Cabell, in 1927; Warren McNeill's Cabellian Harmonics, in 1928; Carl Van Doren's James Branch Cabell, in 1932; and Louis Rubin's study of both Glasgow and Cabell, called No Place on Earth, in 1959. There have been, too, several masters' theses and doctoral dissertations devoted to the work of James Branch Cabell.

To date, however, there has been no really definitive treatment of Cabell for the reason implied by Carl Van Doren in his review of Something about Eve for the Nation in 1927--the sheer enormity of the task. Van Doren said at that time that every treatise that had so far tried to interpret Cabell had been "too slight for its purposes." Furthermore, he explained that when a commentary on Cabell is written, it "must be a packed extensive work, an insolent dictionary, a delicate encyclopedia. It must contain dissertations on the Cabellian geography, chronology, metaphysic, and critical doctrine. It must abstract the plots, analyze the characters and trace them from book to book and subtly, stubbornly interpret the symbolism." He added that "any commentator stubborn enough to do the work demanded is almost certain not to be subtle enough. And any commentator subtle enough will have creative plans sufficient to keep his hands busy. The best that can presumably be hoped for is that somewhere there will occur a writer with all the insight and none of the personal ambition possible to his tribe, and that he will take up what his reviewers will be sure to call, though he must of course blush at the term, a labor of love."[3]

Cabell himself was, of course, fully aware of the flood of notices about him and his work which were appearing all over the nation. He kept huge, black scrapbooks which he filled to overflowing with clippings from newspapers obtained from a clipping bureau to which he subscribed. By means of his scrapbooks he was able to keep his finger on the pulse of the nation and to observe every fluctuation in public favor and taste, as assiduously as any investor on the stock market.

While Cabell was busily spending his Sunday afternoons filling up scrapbook after scrapbook of the world's opinion of him, what attention was Richmond paying to this native son of hers who had become a prominent figure on both the national and the international scene?

Mrs. Eudora Ramsay Richardson, in a most informative article called "Richmond and Its Writers," which appeared in The Bookman in December, 1928, gave some indication of the situation in Richmond in contrast to that in the nation as a whole. She told the story of a near cousin of Cabell's who, upon returning from a trip to New York, is said to have telephoned Mrs. Cabell in great excitement because she had seen something about James in a New York paper. Mrs. Richardson added, "Instead of being the least irritated that members of his family had not yet discovered that his fame had spread abroad, Mr. Cabell was intensely amused."[4]

Twenty-one years later a reporter for the Richmond Times-Dispatch showed that the situation in Cabell's own family had not improved much, for he quoted one of Cabell's near kin as saying, "I wouldn't want James to know it, but his books don't make sense to me, so I long ago stopped trying to read them."[5] It must have hurt Cabell, too, that his first wife never read what he had written, although, he was quick to admit, she defended his privacy unceasingly and was almost embarrassingly delighted when anyone praised his books.

The contrast between the amount of attention paid to him by his own family and that by the world at large must have struck Cabell forcibly. That he was not so much "amused" by this neglect as Mrs. Richardson indicated is revealed in Straws and Prayer-Books, where he wrote rather pathetically: ". . . the persons about whom alone I really care will never read whatever I may elect to publish, nor ever, if by unforeseeable circumstances compelled to read me, could they take my nonsense seriously."[6]

Cabell's feeling that he was being grossly neglected by the city of Richmond must have been accentuated when he realized that his work was never discussed at the monthly literary luncheons of the Woman's Club, to which his wife had presented a set of his books, beautifully autographed in her husband's careful handwriting.7 He is said, too, to have ceased attending the meetings of the Virginia Writers' Club--although he was its first president--because the members never discussed his books.

Still another piece of evidence which seems to point to the fact that the average Richmonder was almost completely indifferent to Cabell, in the years when his popularity was at its height elsewhere, is provided in an article which appeared in the New York World on November 20, 1927. This article stated, perhaps somewhat erroneously, that "James Branch Cabell is happy though ignored in Richmond," and then went on to say, "When outsiders ask questions, the pleasant, wellbred voices of Virginians reply: 'I suppose Mr. Cabell is a great writer, but he's above our level,' or 'Oh, his family's all right,' or 'We consider the great writers of Virginia to be Thomas Nelson Page and Mary Johnston, and--yes, Ellen Glasgow,' or again, 'You just don't hear much about James Branch Cabell.'"

It must have been the accumulation of such situations and incidents as these that finally led Cabell to write with acerbity in his later books about the state of letters in Virginia.

In Let Me Lie Cabell indicated what he thought was the cause of the indifference of his own people towards his work. He thought that it arose from a basic antagonism toward the arts, which he believed had prevailed in Richmond, even as far back as Dickens' famous visit to the city some one hundred years before. At that time, the businessmen of Richmond, according to Cabell, had assured the visiting dignitary at a "petite souper" held in his honor that "they looked forward with an unanimous eagerness to reading several of his books next summer, at the Springs, when one would have leisure for novels." In fact, "one patron of culture" told Dickens "beamingly" how much he had enjoyed Mr. Dickens' Last Days of Pompeii.8

On that memorable occasion, too, Mr. Thomas Ritchie, the editor of the Richmond Enquirer, apologized for not having any "Washington Irving to grace the chair" nor "Bryant . . . to celebrate his praises in rapturous strains," by explaining that "the forte of the Old Dominion is to be found in the masculine production of her statesmen, her Washington, her Jefferson, and her Madison, who have never indulged in works of imagination, in the charms of romance, or in the mere beauties of the belles lettres." "The exact trick of it," Cabell noted, "lies in that 'mere.'"9

Richmond, wrote Cabell in Let Me Lie, had "disapproved of young Mr. Poe because he did not adhere to a code customary among the well-bred. He was, in a word--a word which throughout Virginia, still remains all-damnifying, without having any precise definition--'tacky.'"10

One of Cabell's most bitter criticisms of Virginia's attitude toward the "belles lettres" was expressed in Special Delivery, where, in the course of writing in an irate fashion of the preference of Southern statesmen for the bombastic spoken word rather than for the more solid written word, he said:

> There were no written words to outlive their babblings, for Virginia did not read, nor did she honor any writer. She doted only upon the big words which the aspiring candidates bellowed, or which gray little men with chin whiskers declaimed weepingly from the platform or from the pulpit. She honored stucco idols. She honored mush. No honest writer might thrive in Virginia. There was no art of any kind in Virginia. There was an endless braying. All these things did I behold there in the days of my youth: nor are these ills yet dulcified, to express the matter just as mildly as possible.11

In Let Me Lie Cabell offered an explanation as to why Virginia "did not elect to excel in the polite arts." It was that they did not pay. He added, "Such, rather more exaltedly worded, has been our excuse."12

But, of course, there are two sides to every question. Actually, Cabell was not so completely neglected in Virginia as he thought he was. An active member of the Virginia Writers' Club in the early twenties, the time when Cabell was president of the group, said that people did read Cabell a great deal in Richmond and they did discuss his books, but not in his presence, because Cabell was supersensitive. Cabell, therefore, might never have been aware of these discussions which did take place and which were often of a quite serious nature.

In spite of Mr. Cabell's conviction that he was an outcast in Virginia, there seems to have been quite a Cabell cult in Richmond among the intelligentsia, much as there was on the national level, just after the banning of <u>Jurgen</u>. Naturally, the four young editors of the <u>Reviewer</u>, Hunter Stagg, Margaret Freeman (the present Mrs. Cabell), Emily Clark, and Mary Dallas Street, read Cabell with intelligence and discernment. Furthermore, Mrs. Richardson told how she used to lie awake at night trying to think of clever things to say the next time she saw Cabell in the city library. She wrote, "Then when I do see him standing before a bookshelf I am as awed as I could be if Shakespeare had risen from the dead. So I say, 'How do you do, Mr. Cabell?' and he says, 'How do you do?' very politely, and I pretend that I came to the library merely to find a book."13

It was difficult, however, for Richmonders to be fans of Cabell, even if they did sincerely appreciate his work, for, like many writers and scholars who crave adulation, he wanted it on his own terms. When admirers did summon up enough courage to make a pilgrimage to the shrine of the great man, they would probably find themselves satirized in one of his next books, such as <u>Special Delivery</u> or <u>Smirt</u>, for having invaded his privacy in the first place and then for having asked him stupid and irrelevant questions. Naturally, they would be ashamed and embarrassed at their temerity. One of the best samples of Cabell's mocking attitude toward his callers is provided by a passage from <u>Smirt</u>, the portrait of the artist as a young man: "Thereupon came bustling into Smirt's temple [Cabell's study] Tom, and Dick, and Harry, along with Madam Quelquechose and Señora Etcetera and Lady Ampersand, and after these came Anon and Ibid and the world and his wife, and Mrs. Murgatroyd came also."14

And then Cabell mimicked the idiotic and superfluous questions which these well-meaning, but misguided, creatures inevitably put to him:

"Do you compose on the typewriter? Do you dictate? And do you write in the morning or in the evening?"

"Is alcohol injurious, and are we, or are we not, upon the verge of a vast spiritual awakening?"

"Tell us frankly which one of your own books do you like the best?"

"What about correspondence courses in short story writing, who is your favorite author, and ought children to be taught to believe in Santa Claus? Why is the American Spectator? Do you write every day or do you wait for inspiration to move you?"

"What, Smirt, are your religious beliefs in not over two hundred words? What constitutes your ideal of true womanhood? When is your next book to appear and what are you going to call it?"[15]

Yet, if an admirer really did attempt to ask Cabell a serious question about his work, he was brushed off rather summarily. When an Englishman wrote to Cabell, asking him the meaning of two symbols which Cabell frequently used--his mirror and his two white pigeons-- Cabell said that he would tell the Englishman the answers to his questions when the latter would explain to Cabell why an American should have so much difficulty in getting permission to use the books in the British Museum.[16]

The Richmond press tried to cover Cabell's work conscientiously throughout the years. There are, at the present time, in the morgue of the News Building in Richmond sixty-three newspaper articles from 1928 to 1958 devoted exclusively to James Branch Cabell. There were, actually, through these years, more articles in the papers than there are, at the present time, reposing in the little brown envelope in the newspaper files. The morgue does not have in its collection, for instance, an invaluable key to all of Cabell's work, a short story called "The Journey," published by Cabell in the Times-Dispatch on January 31, 1932. Moreover, from the appearance of Cabell's first short stories, which were published in Harper's Magazine, just after the turn of the century up to the year 1928, there were reviews in the papers which have evidently been discarded by the News librarians, an action which provides in itself, perhaps, a tacit, if withal ironical, commentary on Richmond's attitude towards one of its most illustrious citizens. There had been, too, a number of articles in the Richmond Evening Journal (a paper which sold out to the Times-Dispatch in 1923) which are not in the files in the News Building.

The reviewers of the Richmond newspapers were, in the main commendatory, although they usually confined themselves to merely summarizing the plot of the novel in question and to making a few flattering comments on the style of the author. Although the criticism of some of them, such as that of Hunter Stagg and Warren McNeill, was quite penetrating, comparing favorably in quality with that of the Saturday Review of Literature or of the New York Times, they seem to have hesitated to make any derogatory remarks for fear of offending Cabell. Their reviews were rarely given places of prominence, however, but were usually buried in one of the back pages of the paper, perhaps even among the social items. To an author such as Cabell who felt that he was carving order out of God's chaos, this treatment of his divine creation smacked almost of blasphemy.

Cabell felt, in short, that the Richmond press was not according him the right amount or the right kind of attention. He wrote irritably in Smirt concerning the interviewers sent out by the Times-Leader, his ironical condensation of the names of Richmond's two leading newspapers:

> . . . under varying surnames, and wearing slightly different very young faces, you have called on me aforetime, very, very often, at the bidding of one or another of the local papers. Your questions, during the last twenty-five years have varied in their objectives, but never in their depth and seriousness and futility. Nor indeed have they varied widely. Not ever, for example, during the last twenty-five years, has any representative of the Virginia press failed to inquire, "What will be the future trend of literature in the South?" and "Whom do you consider to have the most promising future among our young Southern writers?"[17]

The questions of these young literary lights were

scarcely better than those of Anon and Ibid. What
Cabell deplored was the fact that few of his Virginian
callers seemed to have read his books thoughtfully or
to have gained any appreciation of those qualities of
his which he deemed the most outstanding--his style,
his wit, his humour, and his irony.

Cabell was, therefore, probably justified in his
annoyance at the neglect of Richmonders, an attitude
which he partly engendered himself by his truculency.
Most of them did seem to ignore him unconscionably,
although there was the little coterie of intellectuals
who were proud of him, who did read his books, and who
did try to show him some attention. The press usually
treated Cabell courteously, if somewhat perfunctorily,
for, after all, a reviewer must be fairly tactful when
he is likely to meet the subject of his article on the
street or in the library at any time.

"Foreigners"--that is, non-Virginians both in this
country and abroad--could afford to be more frank in
their criticism, for they had the advantage of remoteness. It is, therefore, from their reviews that we can
best determine the specific reasons why many people,
Northerners and Southerners alike, did not read Cabell's
books; and it is from Cabell's answers to their criticism,
especially, that we can best determine the effect of the
barbs of critics upon the sensitive soul of the artist.

In 1920 Hugh Walpole made a statement which summed
up neatly the state of affairs which had always existed
between Cabell and his critics. He wrote in "The Art
of James Branch Cabell," published in the Yale Review:
"Let it be said at once that Cabell's art will always
be a sign for hostilities. Not only will he remain, in
all probability, forever alien to the general public,
but he will also, I suspect, be to the end of time a
cause for division among cultivated and experienced
readers."[18] Critics have always differed widely in
their evaluation of Cabell. Opinions have varied from
Hugh Walpole's enthusiastic eulogy of Jurgen, when he
first discovered Cabell--"If Americans are looking for
a book to show to Europe, here it is"[19]--to a comment
which a Times-Dispatch reporter found written in "an
anonymous, old-fashioned handwriting" in a copy of Straws
and Prayer-Books in the Richmond Public Library--"Much
ado about nothing."[20]

Although many critics during the twenties hailed
Cabell as the most eminent American novelist of the time

because of his "wit," his "urbanity," his "poetic style," and his "literary gusto,"[21] many others found him almost unreadable because of what seemed to them to be his "affected" style, his obscurity, his indecencies, his lack of originality, and his egotism. When the latter gave voice to their objections, Cabell sprang to his own defense, adopting ingenious literary devices to meet their attacks. Sometimes he parodied the remarks of his critics; sometimes he merely wrote prefaces or essays to explain his ideas; sometimes he composed neat little parables. At times, adopting the technique of eighteenth-century polemicists, such as Pierre Bayle, Voltaire, and Diderot, he made effective use of footnotes; often he simply inserted his rejoinders in his novels; and, occasionally, he published a sampling of the derogatory reviews which he had received about a given book in the appendix at the end of a subsequent edition, as if to demonstrate to posterity the stupidity of twentieth-century Philistia. One can detect in these many devices the bitterness and frustration of the author masquerading under an assumed air of nonchalance.

Perhaps the remarks of critics which wounded Cabell the most were hostile comments about his style, for he had always prided himself on "writing perfectly of beautiful happenings." Adverse criticism in this quarter must have been all the more difficult for him to bear in view of the fact that in the early days of his writing career his style was judged by those who could read him at all to be one of his most commendable features. All sorts of extravagant terms, such as "needle-point tapestries, delicate laces, intricate embroideries in language" were used to describe Cabell's creations.[22] One of the greatest tributes of all paid to Cabell's style in his heyday was that of a Richmonder, Warren McNeill, who proved in his book <u>Cabellian Harmonics</u> that Cabell's prose is so poetic that parts of it can actually be scanned.[23]

But, with the growth of realism, tastes changed. Hemingway's sparse, clipped sentences became the fad; Cabell's style, by contrast, seemed fussy and cloying. Both Richmonders and outsiders found themselves bored by his affectations. A writer for the <u>Times-Dispatch</u> pounced with glee upon an article in the <u>Bookman</u> in which the author, Harlan Hatcher, declined "to admit that Mr. Cabell is a good story teller or a writer of 'well-nigh perfect prose' or a creative mind or a poet of parts or a guide to the 'golden realm of Apollo.'"[24] A critic for the Nation wrote: "The crystal bowl of his phrasing is still iridescent, but the water in it has become definitely stale with long use."[25]

Cabell's little literary crotchets and mannerisms which had appealed to the sweet, insipid "teens" of the century seemed intolerable to a cynical, disillusioned generation which had been through two world wars and a depression. In 1942 a reviewer for the Saturday Review of Literature seemed annoyed by Cabell's habitual use of such phrases as "not ever" in place of "never," and "by ordinary" in place of "ordinarily."[26] Edd Parks in The Southern Renascence objected to Cabell's use of such phrases as "the tale tells" and to his habit of beginning almost every sentence with a connective so that sentences might seem to flow together. He noticed, too, that Cabell repeated with little or no variation key words, sentences, and even whole paragraphs. While Parks realized that this repetition was used purposely by Cabell to produce a rounded effect, yet Parks found it "unsatisfactory" at times.[27]

To answer remarks of this type concerning his style, Cabell very fittingly chose parody as a weapon. A superb example of his skill in this technique is provided by a review, which he published in the Times-Dispatch, of his own book These Restless Heads, in which, with almost diabolical cleverness, he parodied his own style in order to imitate the remarks of his critics. He said, for example, of his own rhetorical devices, such as his repetitions and his planned alliterations:

> The author of "These Restless Heads" seems to me regrettably overprone to dabble in rhetorical floriculture. I note, for example, his reiteration of the refrain word "nonsense" at the close of each section of the book, and a kindred juggling with "contentment" in the coda of the sections. . . . I observe such unrestrained instances of onomatopoeia as "this flag's fleet, unflagging, flippity-flop flagging." . . . I regard the elaborate building up of long rhapsodies and tirades in order that the instant they reach completion their architect may tumble them over, fleeringly. . . . It seems to me that the author of "These

Restless Heads" has wasted a great deal of
effort upon his filigree niceties. Such
rhetorical love knots are at odds with the
taste of our plain age . . .[28]

Although Cabell did prune from his later work some
of the worst of his "finicky pretensions,"[29] as he
called his preciosities in Some of Us, he never ridded
himself of them completely, for, after all, as Buffon
had said, "Le style est l'homme même."

Of course, the chief reason that people did not
read Cabell was that given by his near kinsman--his books
"just didn't make sense to them." Throughout most of his
writing career Cabell did seem to take what Parks called
"a perverse delight" in confounding his readers.[30]
Carl Van Doren in 1927 had written: "The various intro-
ductions to his works are not enough" to understand
Cabell. "Even his own Scholia merely tantalize, with
their lineages and ground plans and . . . their dexterous
evasions."[31] A reviewer for the Atlantic Monthly said
in 1947 that the reader will frequently resent the necessity of keeping a dictionary, an encyclopedia, and an
atlas within reach.[32]

Cabell did have a way of teasing and tormenting his
readers most unmercifully. Like certain other writers
of his age, such as James Joyce and T. S. Eliot, he used
all sorts of devices designed to challenge to the utmost
the reader's powers of ratiocination. He used allegory,
symbolism, countless allusions, foreign terms, and hundreds of anagrams. His anagrams constitute an interest-
ing study in themselves. Some of them are based on
English words; some, on foreign words; some, on a combination of the two; and some are based on foreign words
with English spellings.

Although many people, according to Cabell in Special
Delivery, did write to him to ask for explanations of
his anagrams, or of his allusions,[33] very few of Cabell's
critics, amateur or professional, tried really seriously
to decipher his code in its entirety. Occasionally, a
few made partial attempts. Mrs. Richardson told of a
group in Richmond who, one Sunday afternoon, tried to
solve the anagrams in Something about Eve. Finally, one
young woman, whose name was Flannagan, was appointed to
call Cabell to find out whether or not any of the anagrams
were formed from foreign words. She gave her name as Ann
Flagan, "to play the anagrammatist's own game," as

Mrs. Richardson said, and learned that all of the anagrams in this particular book are of English origin.[34] In 1928 James Cover prepared a sort of dictionary of Jurgen;[35] but, as yet, no one has had the courage to prepare the "insolent dictionary" or the "delicate encyclopedia," which Van Doren called for in 1927.

In spite of the difficulty which Cabell must have known he was causing his readers, he continued to play his little word games throughout the twenties and the thirties, largely because they were a means whereby he could ridicule the stupidity of humanity with comparative safety. He knew well enough that those who could decipher his code would already be in partial agreement with him, or would be, at least, receptive to his words. The others would have disagreed with him so violently, if they had understood him, that they would have subjected him to even more "persecution" than he had had already. Furthermore, he was loath to divulge his little secrets, such as the meaning of the mirror and the two white pigeons, because, as he wrote in Special Delivery, they gave him "a smug sense of superiority."[36]

The ambivalence of Cabell's attitude toward his public is here once more apparent. Just as he had wanted adulation, but was, at the same time, scornful of those who did try to pay homage to him, so he was simultaneously contemptuous of people because they did not understand his books and annoyed with those who questioned him about his meaning. It must have irritated Cabell, too, that those whom he deemed especially capable of understanding his message seemed either unaware of what he was about, or, what was worse, indifferent to what he had to say.

Still another feature of Cabell's work which was obnoxious to many people, and especially to Virginians, was his "offensiveness," his "lewdness," his "lasciviousness," and his "indecency," as the indictment against Jurgen put the matter on January 6, 1920.[37]

Even as early as The Eagle's Shadow in 1904 Cabell had shown a slight disposition to épater le bourgeois when he had a well-brought-up young lady of an old Virginia family say under great provocation the word "Damn." As the years rolled by and Cabell's work did not receive as much attention as he wished, he must have grown increasingly exasperated. If he could not gain an audience by writing "perfectly of beautiful happenings," he must have thought that perhaps he could gain a following by "writing perfectly of unbeautiful happenings." At least, this is a possible explanation of Cabell's use of questionable material suggested by Hunter Stagg in the Times-Dispatch in 1923.[38] At any rate, such words as staff, lance, and veil are scattered throughout Jurgen with obvious double entendre.

On January 14, 1920, the hue and cry began. John S. Sumner, the agent for the New York Society for the Suppression of Vice, entered the offices of the Robert M. McBride publishing company and seized the plates and unsold copies of the book. Writers all over the United States sprang to the defense of Cabell. Cabell's name became a household word. Even as late as 1935 Mae West listed him among the seven men that she would most like to have "Come up 'n see me sometime." She said that "she would like to find out 'if his books really meant what she thinks they do.'"[39] For two years the case languished on the docket, because more pressing criminal matters had to be attended to.

A brief was prepared for the defense of Jurgen, in which Cabell's hand is evident. The defense was based on the contention that Jurgen is a piece of literature, for it has a theme, sustains a thought, and criticizes life. Its purpose is not, therefore, pornographic. The brief maintained, moreover, that the passages which were singled out as being especially objectionable are not indecent, if read in context. Furthermore, if the passages cited by the New York Society for the Suppression of Vice were considered improper, then many similar passages in the greatest literature of all times, such, for example, as the Bible and Shakespeare, would have to be classified in the same manner.[40]

In connection with this case, Cabell published two amusing little parables--The Taboo in Literature[41] and Jurgen and the Tumblebug.[42] In the former, Cabell joshed Philistia for permitting no mention to be made of one of the absolutely fundamental processes of life--he called this process "eating" in his tale--but, of course, the reader can easily fathom the euphemism. Jurgen and the Tumblebug is a running dialogue between Jurgen (Cabell) and the tumblebug (John S. Sumner). The latter boasts that he has protected Philistia from the invasion of the makers of literature. He says:

> . . . In Philistia to make literature and to make trouble for yourself are synonomous, . . . I know, for already we of Philistia

have been pestered by three of these makers of literature. Yes, there was Edgar [Poe], whom I starved and hunted until I was tired of it; then I chased him up a back alley one night and knocked out those annoying brains of his. And there was Walt [Whitman], whom I chivvied and battered from place to place and made a paralytic out of him; and him, too, I labeled offensive and lewd and lascivious and indecent. Then, later, there was Mark [Twain], whom I frightened into disguising himself in a clown's suit, so that nobody might suspect him of being one of those vile makers of literature; indeed, I frightened him so that he hid away the greater part of what he had made until he was dead and I could not get at him. . . ."

"Nay, but these three," cried Jurgen, "are the glories of Philistia and of all that Philistia has produced, it is these three alone, whom living yet made least of, that today are honored wherever art is honored, and where nobody bothers one way or the other about Philistia!"

"What is art to me and my way of living?" replied the tumblebug wearily. "I have no concern with art and letters and the other lewd idiots of foreign nations. I have in charge the moral welfare of my young, whom I roll here before me, and trust, with St. Anthony's aid, to raise in time to be God-fearing tumblebugs like me. For the rest I have never minded dead men being well spoken of; . . . Meanwhile, I am paid to protest that living persons are offensive and lewd and lascivious and indecent, and one must live."

Jurgen now looked more attentively at this queer creature; and he saw that the tumblebug was malodorous certainly, but at bottom honest and well meaning; and that seemed to Jurgen the saddest thing he had found among the Philistines. For the tumblebug was sincere in his insane doings and all Philistia honored him sincerely, so that there was nowhere any hope for this people.[43]

On October 11, 1922, the case finally came to trial, and the book was acquitted. The decision of the judge, Charles C. Nott, was that the objectionable passages are "delicately conveyed and the whole atmosphere of the story is of such an unreal and supernatural nature that even these suggestions [of indecency] are free from the evils accompanying suggestiveness in more realistic works. In fact, it is doubtful if the book could be read or understood at all by more than a very limited number of readers."[44]

Richmond's reaction to this affair was divided, as always. On the one hand, the <u>Richmond Evening Journal</u> came loyally to the defense of Cabell. Samuel T. Clover, the president and editor of the newspaper, ran an article which began somewhat grandiloquently: "To those privileged mortals who have read Mr. James Branch Cabell's "Jurgen" pronounced by leading critics of the country the most original as well as the most artistic bit of creative literature America has known in years, the seizure of the unsold copies by the New York authorities on the charge of pruriency preferred by the Society for the Suppression of Vice, is one of the colossal absurdities of the age."[45]

This opinion was not held by all Richmonders, however. Mrs. Richardson in her article for the <u>Bookman</u> wrote that when Carl Van Doren, speaking before the Women's Club, had acclaimed <u>Jurgen</u> as "the greatest American novel by a contemporary" and then waited for the applause, "the stillness was at first unbearable. Then [she wrote] applause trickled through the auditorium like sleet upon trees in January. Mr. Cabell, a guest for the afternoon, sat in the front row. The back of his neck grew very red. The audience had not meant to be rude or unappreciative of the honor conferred upon its city. They just couldn't be certain that it was proper to applaud a book that surely was not nice or it wouldn't have been banned."[46]

And, yet, according to the <u>Richmond Times-Dispatch</u>, the demand for <u>Jurgen</u> became so great that in New York "bootleggers" sold copies for as much as fifty dollars.[47] Even in staid little Richmond, copies of <u>Jurgen</u> were sometimes sold for as high as fifteen or twenty dollars.[48]

It was this hypocrisy of humanity that irritated Cabell and that caused him to season his work liberally throughout the rest of his life with dashes of impropriety. Like Voltaire, who is said to have snickered in his study for a lifetime over the little indecencies of La Pucelle, so Cabell took an unholy glee in shocking the smug citizens of Philistia. He knew, as he said in Some of Us, that "in certain biological functions all mankind are very vitally interested," in spite of all pretensions to the contrary. In fact, he wrote that, if there is "one lonely hint of the technically 'indecent,' in any work, it is that single passage which the mentally immature, howsoever staid and gray, will remember whether with sniggers or with indignation, long after the rest of the book is forgotten." He said, too, that because people will go on searching through "unremuneratively chaste reading" in search of "erotica," "many worthless books survive" and become "classics."[49] And then the irrepressible Cabell commiserated impishly with the poor reader for getting "in the way of indecency so very little for his trouble."[50]

Cabell was accused, too, of a lack of originality. In 1921 Richard Le Gallienne, writing for the New York Times, accused him of being a "master of pastiche," of masquerading in other men's ideas.[51]

Cabell did use shreds and patches of other people's concepts. For example, he borrowed the high place from the Bible, Helen of Troy from Homer, Anaitas from Persian mythology, Koshchei from Russian fairy tales, Coth's big flame in Hell from Dante, and the black dog from Goethe. But then Cabell had good precedent for this pilfering. Writers have always borrowed from one another. A part of Genesis is based on the Gilgamesh epic; Virgil used material from Homer and Apollonius of Rhodes; Dante borrowed from Virgil and Boethius; Chaucer borrowed from Dante; Milton borrowed from the Bible, from the Greeks, and from Dante; Shakespeare borrowed from Plutarch; Goethe borrowed from Job, Dante, and Marlowe. The only prerequisite to this artistic plagiarism is that the artist must put his own stamp upon what he writes. This Cabell most certainly did. The only trouble was that he used the same stamp too often.

Cabell's means of answering Richard Le Gallienne, as it was of replying to Henry Seidel Canby and other prominent critics who had written derogatory reviews of him, was to reduce the offender to the status of a footnote. Richard Le Gallienne's footnote identified that worthy gentlemen as being "an English writer of some promise under the latter years of Victoria's reign."[52] By this means, Cabell managed to achieve an effect in time similar to that which might be gained in the physical world by looking through the wrong end of a telescope. He managed to communicate the impression that after immense eons of time had passed, those critics who knew so well how to write would be dredged up from the mire of human memory only with the greatest of difficulty, while Cabell's work would go flourishing down through the centuries like a green bay tree.

Cabell's obscurity, his obscenity, and his lack of originality sprang perhaps from his hurt ego. He seemed to have become so much obsessed by the lack of human comprehension that he filled his later books with endless laments concerning the stupidity of mankind, the intellectual isolation of the author, and the inevitable extinction of the ego—especially of his own identity.

Edd Parks in The Southern Renascence said that later comments on his "humanistic aesthetic" became so egocentric and irritable" that he seemed to have "lost sight of his work in his self-concern for the artist."[53] Granville Hicks in The Great Tradition called him a "sleek, smug egotist."[54] An unidentified reviewer of Ladies and Gentlemen in the Saturday Review of Literature wrote of him in 1934: "Mr. Branch Cabell . . . is devoting those years which he himself declared to be declining, to the carving of cherrystones, the cultivation of cattishness, and the paying off of old grudges."[55]

The works in which Cabell's egotism is the most apparent are his fictitious letters contained in Special Delivery, his later novels, especially Smirt, his diatribe against Virginia, Let Me Lie, and his autobiography, As I Remember It.

Of course, by the publication of these works Cabell did incur the resentment of a great many people. A Richmond reporter who called himself a "victim" of one of Cabell's "specials" answered back in the Times-Dispatch for June 18, 1933, in a letter which is almost as much a masterpiece of satire as Cabell's own works. Some sample gleanings from this letter are:

> You are quite correct in terming this enforced tête-à-tête something for which neither of us is in any way responsible, . . . Time was when, fresh out of college and fired by adolescent admiration of the 'author of Jurgen' I went to my first interview with you as if on some high romantic quest.. . . . Then I trembled with somewhat the same perturbation that shook

Heine as he approached his meeting with
Goethe, and I quite forgot all the questions which you had expected me to ask
and which you nevertheless answered without the asking. . . . But since, my dear
sir, I have interviewed such leviathans
of news as politicians, felons, feminists
and authors better known to our readers
than you are, this periodical call on the
late James Branch Cabell leaves me, unaccountably unmoved.[56]

Cabell, for his part, felt that it was next to
impossible to please his critics, especially his
Southern critics. The Almighty himself, he was sure,
could not accomplish that insuperable task. In Smirt
Cabell created an ironic situation in which he presented
his little earthling, who, of course, is Cabell himself,
conversing with the great Creator of the Universe.
While the two are reposing comfortably on billowy clouds,
Cabell has the "All-Highest," as he calls God in this
book, ask his visitor in a timid, halting manner whether
it might not be a good idea for the heavenly penman to
revise his book--the Holy Bible--to bring it up to date,
so that it might be more in line with modern theology.
Smirt shudders from personal experience at such a proposal, for he feels, much as a father would, that he must
protect this creation of his "from the cruel and silent
derision" which he is certain "would incur quite inevitably by making any more revelations to mankind in the
present state of American letters."[57] Such a measure
would be especially deplorable in the South, for the
South, because of its persistent anti-intellectualism,
would remain steadfastly "silent and unscornful, not
heeding this book, or any other book."[58]

Judging from available evidence, then, Cabell and
his public both had good reasons for feeling hostile to
each other. Cabell accused humanity of stupidity and
dullness; humanity retaliated by accusing the author of
ineptitude and egotism. Besides, so far as Virginians
were concerned, Cabell had violated the Virginian code of
ethics by putting their little peccadillos into print.

Because Cabell realized in the middle years of his
life that he was out of joint with his neighbors and with
his times he created his medieval kingdom of Poictesme,
where, ostensibly, he would not be writing about Virginia
or even America. If people read Virginia into Poictesme,

<u>they</u> were responsible, not the author. By Poictesme Cabell felt that he could free himself from the accusation that he was dealing with the contemporaneous and with the particular. Poictesme, then, was struck from the abrasion of the critic upon the artist.

Although Cabell has now been swept away by that "impartial wind," about which he wrote so magnificently in "The Journey," along with "the emperors and the dolphins and the aureoled martyrs and the bright . . . heralds and the spruce page boys,"[59] yet the "Biography of the Life of Manuel" remains. Perhaps, ironically enough, the continued bickering of those carping critics who had troubled Cabell in life will be the means of protecting his name in death from the immediate ravages of the prowling old storm god who eventually eradicates all monuments of human endeavor from the minds of men.

NOTES

[1] Vernon Lewis Parrington, "The Incomparable Mr. Cabell," Main Currents in American Thought (New York: Harcourt, Brace and Company, 1930), III, 333-345.

[2] Willard Thorp, American Writing in the Twentieth Century (Cambridge, Massachusetts: Harvard University Press, 1960), pp. 52-54.

[3] Carl Van Doren, review of Something About Eve, Nation, CXXV (October 12, 1927), 386. Since that time James Cover has prepared a sort of dictionary of Jurgen (James P. Cover, Notes on Jurgen [New York: Robert M. McBride & Company, 1928]) and Julius Lawrence Rothman, the editor of a magazine devoted primarily to Cabell and entitled The Cabellian: A Journal of the Second American Renaissance (1968-1972) has compiled an invaluable dictionary entitled "A Glossarial Index to the 'Biography of the Life of Manual,'" unpublished Ph.D. dissertation, Columbia University, 1954. (Available from University Microfilms, Ann Arbor, Michigan.)

[4] Eudora Ramsay Richardson, "Richmond and Its Writers," Bookman XVIII (December, 1928), 450.

[5] Richmond Times-Dispatch, April 10, 1949.

[6] Cabell, Straws and Prayer-Books, Works, XVII, 238.

[7] Richardson, "Richmond and Its Writers," p. 449.

[8] Cabell, Let Me Lie, p. 121.

[9] Ibid., p. 123.

[10] Ibid., p. 131.

[11] Cabell, Special Delivery, p. 53.

[12] Cabell, Let Me Lie, p. 117.

[13] Richardson, "Richmond and Its Writers," p. 450.

[14] Cabell, Smirt, p. 216.

[15] Ibid., p. 220.

[16] Cabell, Special Delivery, pp. 198-212.

[17] Cabell, Smirt, p. 27.

[18] Hugh Walpole, "The Art of James Branch Cabell," Yale Review, IX (July, 1920), p. 687.

[19] Hugh Walpole, quoted in the Richmond Times-Dispatch, January 4, 1920.

[20] Richmond Times-Dispatch, April 10, 1949.

[21] Armistead C. Gordon, Jr., quoted in "Pro and Con Cabell," *Richmond Times-Dispatch*, August 23, 1946.

[22] M. P. Mooney, "Some Rogueries of James Branch Cabell," *A Round-Table in Poictesme*, eds. Don Bregenzer and Samuel Loveman (Cleveland: Privately printed by members of the Colophon Club, 1924), p. 88.

[23] Warren McNeill, *Cabellian Harmonics* (New York: Random House, 1928), *passim*.

[24] Alan Burton Clarke, "On Not Reading James Branch Cabell," *Richmond Times-Dispatch*, March 1, 1931.

[25] J. M. Berryman, review of *Smith*, *Nation*, CXLI (November 28, 1935), 630.

[26] Ben Ray Redman, review of *The First Gentleman of America*, Saturday Review of Literature, XXV (February 7, 1942), 7.

[27] Louis D. Rubin, Jr., and Robert D. Jacobs, eds., *The Southern Renascence* (Baltimore: The Johns Hopkins University Press, 1953), p. 259.

[28] [James] Branch Cabell, "Objections to James Branch Cabell." *Richmond Times Dispatch*, January 31, 1932, Part III, p. 6.

[29] James Branch Cabell, *Some of Us: An Essay in Epitaphs* (New York: Robert M. McBride & Company, 1930), p. 85.

[30] Rubin and Jacobs, *The Southern Renascence,* p. 259.

[31] Carl Van Doren, review of *Something About Eve*, *Nation*, CXXV (October 12, 1927), 386.

[32] William M. Kunstler, review of *Let Me Lie*, *Atlantic Monthly*, CLXXIX (May, 1947), 160.

[33] Cabell, *Special Delivery*, pp. 192-193.

[34] Richardson, "Richmond and Its Writers," p. 450.

[35] Cover, *Notes on Jurgen*. Also Julius Rothman's "A Glossarial Index to the 'Biography of the Live of Manuel,'" See n. 3.

[36] Cabell, *Special Delivery*, p. 193.

[37] Guy Holt, ed., *Jurgen and the Law* (New York: Robert M. McBride & Co., 1923), p. 11.

[38] Hunter Stagg, review of *The High Place*, Richmond Times-Dispatch, December 2, 1923.

[39] Unidentified clipping in the Richmond newspaper file, dated April 8, 1935.

[40] Holt, ed., Jurgen and the Law, passim.

[41] Cabell, "The Taboo in Literature," New York Evening Post, December 11, 1920.

[42] Cabell, "Jurgen and the Tumblebug," Richmond Evening Journal, February 10, 1920, p. 6.

[43] Ibid.

[44] Holt, ed., Jurgen and the Law, p. 13.

[45] Samuel T. Clover, "Jurgen and External Suggestion," Richmond Evening Journal, February 10, 1920, p. 6.

[46] Richardson, "Richmond and Its Writers," p. 449.

[47] Richmond Times-Dispatch, October 20, 1922, p. 1.

[48] "Risqué and Sex Books in Biggest Vogue Here," Richmond News Leader clipping dated only 1922.

[49] Cabell, Some of Us, pp. 80-81.

[50] Ibid., 81.

[51] Richard Le Gallienne, "James Branch Cabell, Master Pastiche," New York Times, February 13, 1920, p. 3.

[52] Cabell, Straws and Prayer-Books, Works, XVII, 269.

[53] Rubin and Jacobs, The Southern Renascence, p. 260.

[54] Granville Hicks, The Great Tradition (New York: Macmillan & Co.), p. 22.

[55] "Dean Letters," Saturday Review of Literature, XI (November 24, 1934), 307.

[56] "One of Cabell's 'Specials' Gets Answered by a Victim," Richmond Times-Dispatch, June 18, 1933.

[57] Cabell, Smirt, p. 64.

[58] Ibid., p. 63.

[59] Cabell, "The Journey," Richmond Times-Dispatch, January 31, 1932, Section III, Part 2, p. 2.

CABELL'S TRANSLATION OF VIRGINIA

Like many Southern writers and intellectuals, James Branch Cabell was faced with a dilemma throughout much of his lifetime. Because of his education, his travels, and his extensive reading, he had developed in his youth a more liberal outlook on life than most of his fellow Virginians. For this reason, he found himself in frequent disagreement with the beliefs and mores of his "neighbors," whose conservative views, he felt, were stifling the development, not only of his art, but also of the society of which he was a part. Since his traffic was in words, he naturally gave voice to his opinions; his fellow citizens, just as naturally, resented his criticism.

The problem with which Cabell was faced came to a head in the middle of the second decade of this century, after he had been writing for almost twenty years. At first, he had turned out romantic little tales and poems concerned with the lives and loves of ladies and gentlemen of the Middle Ages, the Renaissance, the Restoration, and the Eighteenth Century.[1] He had even tried his hand at three novels and one short story laid in his own contemporary Virginia.[2] None of these productions had met with any great success, although his critics did praise his style. What was particularly discouraging to the writer was the indifference of his fellow Richmonders toward his work. So far as he could determine, most of his friends and acquaintances did not read his books at all. If they did read them, they either failed to see any particular merit in what he had written, or, as he became increasingly critical in the "Virginia" novels, they were alienated by his comments. An uneasy relationship developed, therefore, between the writer and the people in his more immediate environment.

In The Rivet in Grandfather's Neck, the last of the three Virginia novels of this early period, Cabell's irritation at the "notions of his neighbors," his pet phrase for the ideas of people with whom he was most frequently associated, burst forth in full force. For example, in a thumb-nail biography of his hero, Colonel Rudolph Musgrave, written in the manner of Who's Who, Cabell referred to Virginia as Sill. (probably a blend of silly and Ill., suggested perhaps by the abbreviation of Illinois). Colonel Musgrave, therefore, had attended the "U. of Sill.," had edited the "Sill. Mag. of Biog.," and was a "mem. exec. bd. of the Sill. Hist. Assn. for the Preservation of Ruins"[3] (the Association for the Preservation of Virginia Antiquities). Like other Southern orators, he delivered pompous after-dinner speeches, in which he spoke about "the stately mansions of the old régime, and about the trampling of gray battalions, and about honeysuckles and bugles and magnolias, and about the feudal magnificence and the generally superb ideals of an older South."[4] In this book, too, Cabell began to deal glancing blows at the Southerners' impossibly idealized view of their womenfolk. Rudolph's "goddess," Patricia Stapylton, who, before her marriage to the Colonel, had seemed to him to be a diaphanous "heap of fluffy frills and ruffles,"[5] appeared, after her marriage, to be an ordinary human being after all. She was quite capable of calling her husband a "jack-ass fool,"[6] and of having an affair with her house guest, John Charteris.

This novel must have created a minor furor in Richmond, judging from an episode called "Prehistorics" in a fable purportedly written by John Charteris, Cabell's auctorial self in his first period. When the hero of this little tale dares to hint to the citizens of Lichfield that their town might be anything less than perfect, they retaliate by throwing paving stones at him.[7]

Since Cabell was a sensitive artist and scholar, rather than a crusader, he must have been disturbed by the disapproval of his fellow citizens. Although he wanted to write about his native state, he did not want to fight about it. Besides, he had his family to consider, for he had married in 1913. He must have felt, much as had his character, Robert Etheridge Townsend,[8] in The Cords of Vanity, that he wanted to write "humorously" about his homeland, but that he could not, for he was too close to his subject; he knew it too well. Besides, he knew that his people were basically like people everywhere.[9] In fact, Cabell knew that he himself was much like his neighbors, for he was a product of the same environment as theirs. He felt, like Townsend, that Lichfield (Richmond) and Fairhaven (Williamsburg) had "got at and into . . . [him] when . . . [he] was too young to defend . . . [himself]" and that he was no more able to separate himself from his "inbred traditions . . . than a carpet could change its pattern."[10] The knowledge that he shared, to some extent, the faults of his neighbors perhaps made Cabell even more annoyed when he saw the exaggeration of his own traits in others.

At the end of the first part of his writing career, he felt that he had to find some means whereby he could write about his own culture in such a way that people of like mind would understand his message, while his more hostile neighbors would remain unaware of what he was doing. Cabell wanted to continue living in Richmond, which was home to him, for he had come of old Richmond families, and, even though he criticized the city and the parts of Virginia with which he was the most familiar, he still loved the area, just as the Biblical prophets had loved Judah and Israel.

At the time when he began working seriously on *The Cream of the Jest*, in 1914, he found some relief from his difficulties by having his writer hero, Felix Kennaston, leave the trials of everyday life in Lichfield and junket off at intervals to Storisende, a city in a country which he had begun fabricating as far back as 1905. At that time, when he was having trouble with the geography of Tunbridge Wells, the setting of a story called "In the Second April," which eventually appeared in *Gallantry* (1907), he had begun to make up purely imaginary places, such as the château of Bellegarde and the Forest of Acaire.[11] He placed these "creations" in the French Midi, an area which had fascinated him since his college days, when he had developed an interest in Provençal poetry.[12] In fact, he had specifically labeled as a "Provençal Burden" the "Castle of Content," the first little poem which he was later willing to publish commercially under his own name.[13] He had used his imaginary country again for "The Scapegoats," another story which appeared in *Gallantry*. It had served him well, too, when he was writing a novel which was eventually named *Domnei*.[14]

While writing *The Cream of the Jest*, Cabell hit upon the way of solving the dilemma which had confronted him since *The Cords of Vanity*. Instead of moving a character, Felix Kennaston, to medieval France, why not translate all of his "neighbors" to that fascinating imaginary country of his, which had been growing through the years? Why not convert the Virginians into the princelings and princesses which they so fondly thought of themselves as being? He wrote in *Let Me Lie* that, after the events at Appomattox, the typical Southerner felt that he was "the defrauded heir to a peerage in the Old South" and that, although he would never admit it, he "should [not] have to work for his living."[15] It was this state of mind, Cabell felt, that was producing a deplorable "indolence" in the South, which, on the intellectual plane, was leading to a sterility of aesthetics, except, as he put it, "in the superb and philanthropic romanticizing of Virginia history."[16] He gave as an example of this intellectual lethargy the fact that in all the long years of its existence, William and Mary (his own alma mater and the King's College of his early "Virginia" novels) had never produced one creative artist, with the exception of Thomas Jefferson.[17] He wrote, too, that the Virginians always looked back to the glories of ante-bellum days. They could never look to the present or to the future.[18]

Cabell had long been of the opinion that there was much that was medieval in the thinking of his native state. In fact, when, as a child, he had heard tales of General Lee and of the splendors of a past that actually never was, he had confused these stories in his mind with the legends of King Arthur and the Knights of the Round Table.[19] Moreover, he had noticed that the code of ethics of medieval society and that of ante-bellum Virginia were much alike for similar reasons. Both had developed hierarchical societies, with God at the apex of the pyramid, his messenger-redeemer-captain just below, the lord and lady of the medieval fief or of the Virginia plantation next, but not too far beneath the first two ranks, and the serfs or slaves at the bottom of the social structure. Because of the nature of their societies, the medieval baron and the Virginia planter each felt that it was his bounden duty to "serve his God, his honor and his lady without any reservation." Furthermore, this ethical trinity was invariably accompanied by "the idea of vicarship: for," Cabell thought, "the chivalrous person is, in his own eyes at least, the child of God, and goes about this world as his Father's representative in an alien country."[20] To some extent, then, every Virginia gentleman is a little "redeemer" in his own right. To preserve this illusion every well-born Virginian automatically perpetuates the myths and the code of behavior of the society into which he has been born. Cabell believed that this impulse was so strong that he wrote in Let Me Lie: ". . . no power in nature can upset the faith of a Virginian of the old school as to the myths among which he was reared, and of which he needs to be worthy. No power can shake his belief in his own eternal rightness. . . . Nor . . . can any known power take away, from the wellborn Virginian, that ever-sustaining sense of moral uplift which he gets out of being chivalrous at no matter what costs to himself, or to other persons either."[21]

Cabell had early begun to question the validity of

Virginia myths. Although he admired General Lee for going off to be president of little Washington College on the other side of the Blue Ridge when he might have had more lucrative positions,22 yet, even as a child, Cabell had noticed the curious discrepancies between public utterances about the great Lee and the private gossip about the little peccadillos of this same seemingly "impeccable" being.23 Cabell eventually came to realize that he had witnessed the phenomenon of a myth in the making. No great man, in actual life, can be as flawless as he is made to be in the tales of those who come after him, for, in later accounts, he is mercifully divested of his human foibles and crotchets. The lack of correspondence between myth and reality led Cabell to speculate about the truth of myths in general. If the great Lee had had little human faults, how about the other great redeemer-captains of history, such as Odysseus, Aeneas, or even Jesus himself? Was the past ever so splendid as people like to imagine it? Should it become a strait jacket to hinder the development of society in the present? Cabell felt that he had to find some means whereby he could become something of an iconoclast, for he had enough of the South in him to feel that he, too, was a vicar and had to watch over the welfare of his people.

Then a brilliant idea must have occurred to Cabell. His medieval country, which he had named "Poictesme," because it had been "born--of an illicit union between Poictiers and Angoulesme,"24 was lying right at hand. Why not use it as a vehicle to satirize the shortcomings of his own society? It seemed to be exactly what he needed. He felt quite sure that his fellow Richmonders would never see themselves as Frenchmen, whereas, with their Cavalier tradition, they might recognize themselves as medieval Englishmen. The translation of Virginia and its ideas to France would provide him with just the amount of disguise that he deemed necessary. Only the ones whom he really wanted to understand would get his point. He would thus have the maximum amount of freedom with the minimum amount of inconvenience. Cabell was sure that he would succeed with his little ruse, and he was completely right. In fact, few people even today seem to realize what he was doing, although Cabell took special care to provide a hint by including both The Cream of the Jest and The Lineage of Lichfield in the same volume of the Storisende Edition of his completed work up until 1930 and by specifically subtitling this volume: Two Comedies of Evasion. What was he escaping from if not his immediate environment? This point is substantiated by the fact that he explains outright in <u>Let Me Lie</u> that <u>Lichfield</u> is Richmond,25 and in <u>Straws and Prayer-Books</u> he further informs his readers that Lichfield was "a <u>suburbs</u>" of Poictesme.26 By <u>suburbs</u> Cabell obviously means the part of a city which comes <u>before</u> the main residential district and not just the "outlying" parts or the "outskirts" of a <u>city</u>. Cabell, here, is blurring spatial and temporal concepts, just as he did in his conversion to a <u>place</u> of Villon's <u>antan</u>, which means simply <u>yesteryear</u> in the "Ballade des dames du temps jadis." If Lichfield is Richmond in his early books, is it not logical to consider Poictesme as a surrogate for his section of Virginia? By making this substitution he is, furthermore, again blurring space and time, for Poictesme is not merely a physical concept, but an ideological one as well; Poictesme is an area where prevails a certain set of ideals peculiar to the former plantation sections of Virginia, as well as to similar parts of the whole South. Cabell's part of Virginia, in fact, much more closely resembles the plantation areas of the Deep South than it does other sections of his own state--such "corrupted" areas as northern Virginia, the sprawling, populous areas around Norfolk, and the "Valley."

Cabell must have entertained himself hugely with his dream world, which was a blend of the two "countries" that he loved best--southern Virginia and southern France. In his travels in Europe as a young man, he must have noticed that the two regions are alike in many respects. Both start with low sandy coastlines, where pine trees are plentiful, and both slope up to mountainous areas, the Blue Ridge in Virginia and the Alps-Jura chain in France. Cabell did not use the mountains which actually border on southern France, however, as can be seen on a map drawn by Frank C. Papé27 of Tunbridge Wells. Instead, he borrowed the little Taunus range, northwest of Frankfurt-am-Main in Germany, named it the Taunenfels, and deposited it in the northern part of his imaginary country, probably to suggest the Germanic origin of the settlers who had streamed from Pennsylvania down into the northern part of the Virginia Valley and the Blue Ridge. Immediately southeast of the Taunenfels, he retained a truncated section of Virginia's Piedmont, which he called the "Piemontais." He kept just enough of it to suggest perhaps that part of Virginia which makes up Albemarle County, the home of Mr. Jefferson and his university. In the north, both areas stop short of their great national capitals, Paris in France and Washington in America. Instead the "capitals" of both countries are located somewhat east of the middle of the "state"--Richmond in Virginia,

Storisende in Poictesme. Storisende also occupies relatively the same position in Poictesme as Lyons in France. Cabell must have been struck by the fact that Lyons had been the home of the Pléiade, a sixteenth-century literary school in France, just as Richmond was the home of Cabell, Ellen Glasgow, and later of the <u>Reviewer</u>. Both sections have old "universities"28 which had been attended by "ribald" writers. France has its Montpellier, where Rabelais had studied, and Virginia, its Williamsburg, where Cabell had received his education. Finally, Poictesme, like Provence, is bordered on the south by a gulf--the Golfe du Lion, a name which must have delighted Cabell, the Master Philologist, for if the word <u>Lion</u> is pronounced in the English manner, it sounds like <u>Lyin</u>', Virginian for <u>Lying</u>. Cabell was of the opinion that Southerners could not and would not face the truth about themselves.

    Not only must Cabell have noticed the similarities between the physical features of southern France and Virginia, but he must have detected the marked spiritual resemblances between the people of the two areas. The natives of both sections are a conservative and devout rural folk. Both sections write history "in the more freely interpretative form of fiction," a phrase which Cabell had borrowed from Ellen Glasgow.29 There are fantastic tales running rife in the French Midi, such as that of the three Marys--Mary Magdalene, Mary Jacobé, and Mary Salomé--who, with a party of six other Christians, came to the shores of southern France in about 40 A.D., after having been set adrift from the Holy Land by enemies of the Christians. Virginia, too, perpetuates its myths without question. It believes that all of the details of the Pocahontas story are completely true, that Jamestown was the first permanent white settlement in America, and that Virginia Dare was the first white child born in the New World.30 The people of both sections like to present a good front to the world. Cabell must have noticed that Provence is the home of that notorious boaster and hunter created by Alphonse Daudet, Tartarin de Tarascon, who, in a sense, has a number of Virginia counterparts. Like Tartarin, rural Virginians love to hunt. They are not given to boasting much about their individual prowess, however, but rather they like to talk about their illustrious ancestors. After all, as Cabell wrote amusedly so many times throughout his work, Virginia prides itself on being the mother of presidents and the cradle of liberty. Every Virginian, therefore, can bask in this reflected glory. Also, Cabell was probably well aware that from a town in the Midi came that famed hero, Cyrano de Bergerac, who was inordinately jealous of his honor. Finally, in both sections there has been throughout the years a sort of "woman worship." The southern part of France was the area especially favored by the troubadours of old, who tried to pick up a livelihood by singing of the beauties and virtues of the fair ladies of the castles. To this day in Arles, which Cabell had made the home of the Princess Alianora in Figures of Earth, can be seen straight, noble-looking old ladies, who, with the removal of the coif and a change in language, would closely resemble the descendants of the plantation mistresses. Moreover, in Virginia there are still annual "tu'naments," culminating in a ball presided over by a Queen of Love and Beauty. All in all, Cabell must have felt that the people of southern Virginia had enough of the qualities of those of southern France to make the transition easy to effect. Both peoples believed in fantastic myths; both had, in their way, a highly developed sense of honor; and both placed their womenfolk on pedestals.

Through all of the books of the middle period, which lasted until the completion of the Storisende Edition of his collected work in 1930, Cabell played with his imaginary country. By his use of Poictesme, he was able to study and evaluate with impunity the myths of his fellow Virginians and their tripartite moral code.

The first part of the ethical trinity which Cabell subjected to a thorough investigation was the Southerners' implicit faith in a personal deity and their desire to serve this being. The reason for his preoccupation with this aspect of Virginia mythology was his belief that his people's "service to God" had degenerated, for the most part, to mere form and ritual.[31] Furthermore, he was annoyed that his neighbors insisted that everyone must agree with their own rather narrow concept of God and their ideas of what constitutes service to this deity. Cabell himself was of the opinion that all "human ideas are probably not ever correct about anything" and that human beliefs are, in the last analysis, simply "playthings" with which one diverts himself "during the night-season of a . . . Walburga's Eve," which is called living.[32] He felt that the two types of people who are especially prone to demand this absolute conformity to their own "notions" are women and priests. The particular "priest" that Cabell probably had in mind, much of the time, was Bishop Cannon, a prelate of the Methodist church, who had contrived to have Prohibition introduced into Virginia before it became a national law in 1920. Not only Cabell but many of the other young liberals of the time were annoyed by the activities of this assiduous churchman.

Because of Cabell's desire to create a greater spirit of tolerance in the South, he attacked four major facets of religion, those to which Fundamentalists are generally the most attached: the belief in a life after death, in which rewards and punishments might, at last, be meted out fairly; the conception of a personal God; the belief in divine emissaries from Heaven; and the infallibility of sacred records.

Perhaps Cabell's best attack on the belief in a life after death is in Jurgen. Because Cabell believed that Heaven and Hell are simply illusions which a child inherits from his ancestors, he called Satan "Grandfather Satan,"[33] and he made Heaven the result of the wishful thinking of Jurgen's grandmother.[34] In Jurgen, Cabell put the hero's father, Coth, into Hell, where he is inclosed in a flame, much as was Odysseus in Dante's Inferno. There, the old curmudgeon exhorts the little demons who attend his flame to build the fire ever higher and higher to satisfy the demands of Coth's own conscience.[35] Cabell attributed Jurgen's grandmother's Heaven, not to God, but to one "Koshchei," who created it to satisfy her desires.[36] Cabell called this being a demiurge, a word which meant to the ancient Greeks "the creator of the material universe" and even sometimes "the creator of evil." The word is derived from the Greek demios, belonging to the people, and ergos, meaning worker or working. Therefore, the word demiurge carries with it the connotation of a being who, though ostensibly working for the people, is not always working for their best interests. With Cabell's penchant for wresting every possible meaning from a word or symbol, he must also have noticed that the two parts of the word demiurge have other and different meanings in two other languages. Demi in French means half, and urge in English is impulse. Thus, the demiurge could also mean a half impulse, or even a half-hearted impulse, which would result in a botched universe. At any rate, even in the life after death this force, which creates "things as they are," does not seem to satisfy Coth completely. In fact, Koshchei's only masterpiece seems to be Jurgen's grandmother's heaven, for to her, alone, he seems to have given complete satisfaction.

Cabell, also, attributed the concept of a very human God--the second aspect of the Southerner's belief--to this same sorcerer-craftsman taken from Russian mythology. For Jurgen's grandmother, because she loved, Koshchei took pains to create a god complete with a rainbow, a harp, cherubim and seraphim, organ music, and all of the other trappings with which her imagination invested him. God himself even admits that he is an illusion of an old woman, as Jurgen had proved so many times.[37]

The third facet of Southern religiosity which Cabell assailed is the belief in a redeemer--someone who will save the people from their misfortunes. Perhaps it is this belief, coupled with the conviction of every well-born Virginian that he, too, is God's representative upon earth, which makes the Southerner venerate his leaders as he does, for his captains must be even more sublime than are the upper-class Virginians themselves. In <u>The Silver Stallion</u> (1926) Cabell set forth a succession of "messengers" who have appeared at regular intervals of six hundred years and who, after their allotted time, have entered alive into Heaven. Since all the great captains are to come again (for the redeemer shades off into the captain), it is highly likely that Manuel, Cabell's own creation, will return to earth.[38] Cabell put the intervals for the appearance of these divine emissaries at six hundred years to suggest, probably, that that long a time had elapsed between Manuel, who had ascended alive into Heaven in 1239, and the great demigod of the South, General Lee.

These recurrent "redeemers," Cabell intimates, if demythologized, would appear to be quite ordinary human beings with the usual human propensities. He develops this theme in two novels, <u>Figures of Earth</u> and <u>The Silver Stallion</u>. In the first of these two books, Cabell created Manuel, probably with the myths of both Jesus and Lee in mind, along with himself and every other being, for that matter, for Cabell knew full well that every individual is a god unto himself in life and is purged of his dross by his associates beyond life. By giving his hero the name <u>Manuel</u>, Cabell could suggest several different shades of meaning. First, he must have had in mind the Hebrew word <u>Emmanuel</u>, which means <u>God is with us</u>. Then, Manuel is also a blend of the English word <u>man</u> and the Hebrew <u>el</u>, meaning God. Little man, therefore, becomes the Man-God. Manuel, like all redeemers, holds this position until he is ironically supplanted by Donander, a member of Manuel's own Fellowship of the Silver Stallion, a group which suggests all groups who rally around great leaders, such as the Twelve Disciples, the Knights of the Round Table, and the brave Confederate battalions who sallied forth against the invading Northmen.

Although Cabell maintains that Southerners are convinced of their own eternal rightness, are they really as infallible as they like to consider themselves? Are they not a mixture of good and evil, just as are all other human beings? Cabell sets forth his opinion on this matter by having his hero, Manuel, racket about Poictesme for a time, during which he repels the Northmen, as the South had tried to do. Although he lives a very human life, he is finally reported by the child Jurgen as having ascended into Heaven.[39] Strangely enough, people believe this preposterous tale told by the child Jurgen to keep himself from being punished for running away from home.[40] Gradually, through the assiduous efforts of Niafer, Manuel's wife, to whom the "redeemer" had been none too faithful, and through the work of Holmendis, her attendant priest, Manuel comes to be considered as the savior of mankind, whose imminent return is eagerly awaited. However, not everyone is of the opinion that Manuel was without fault, for no human beings, not even the redeemers of mankind, are completely blameless. In The Silver Stallion Anavalt, one of Manuel's followers, delivers what appears, in form, to be a "lament" for the departed hero, but rather than being an encomium it is actually a calumniation. The vein of Anavalt's words is somewhat as follows:

> Manuel was cunning. . . . Nobody could outwit Manuel. What he wanted he took, if he could get it that way, with his strong hand: but, if not, he used his artful head and his lazy, wheedling tongue, and his other members, too, so that the person whom he was deluding would give Manuel what he required.[41]

This is strange praise, indeed, for a redeemer-hero, but "redeemers," even the great Lee, do live earthly lives. It is the impossible myth which Cabell was attacking and not the persons themselves.

In the course of ridiculing the belief in the infallibility of God's representatives upon earth, Cabell managed to inject a note, which, by implication at least, dealt with the fourth aspect of the South's religiosity--the belief of the Bible Belt that Holy Writ had been handed down to mankind exactly as it had been composed by the hand of God. One of his most successful, though somewhat oblique, examples of the kind of accident which can occur in the transmission of records appears in his account of the deification of the resurrected heathen, Saint Hoprig, the patron saint of Florian de Puysange of The High Place (1923). St. Hoprig, whose name is probably a blend of the French word haut, meaning high, tall, or great, and the English word prig, had somewhat ruthlessly liquidated two Christian missionaries, Ork and Horrig (horrid prig?),

who had been wandering about Poictesme making converts.
Although there was not enough left of Ork to bury, the
remains of Horrig were interred, and a tomb, inscribed
with his name, was erected over his grave. When the tail
of the first R in Horrig's name became blurred with the
passage of time, the people thought that the tomb was
that of Hoprig. When miracles occurred at the tomb, they
mistakenly canonized the <u>heathen</u> Hoprig, rather than the
<u>Christian</u> Horrig.42

Cabell usually represented his "saints"--among whom
the wellborn Virginians would certainly include themselves--
as being not much better than the generality of men. For
instance, they are not always particularly chaste. Cabell
was of the opinion that in the evening, when the lights are
turned low, indiscretions may be committed in the back parlors of even the best Richmond homes. St. Hoprig, therefore, like many another of God's "representatives" upon
earth, begat a child upon Melior, the heroine of <u>The High
Place</u>, ostensibly so that Melior and Florian de Puysange,
her husband, would not produce a child whom Florian had
already promised to Janicot, the devil, as payment for his
aid in securing Melior for Florian, in the first place.
Although St. Hoprig's reason may seem commendable, yet
when Florian learns of this collusion between his wife and
his priest, he is shocked at the alliance of "beauty and
holiness . . . to avoid offending against the notions of
the neighbors."43 There is slightly more than a hint, too,
that Holmendis in <u>The Silver Stallion</u> might become Manuel's
successor in Niafer's bedroom.44

So much for the religiosity of the South. Yet, even
though Cabell felt that the beliefs of his people were
impossible to verify and that religious worship had degenerated to a meaningless jargon and ritual, he does present
Jurgen as remembering with affection the simple faith of
his elders, and he is truly sorry that he cannot believe
in the God of his grandmother.45

The second part of Virginia's ethical trinity was the
feeling of the Southern aristocrat that his own individual
honor, as well as that of his whole class, must be protected at all costs. Throughout his books, Cabell's message is that since human beings cannot or will not attain
perfection, they concentrate upon the mere <u>appearance</u> of
excellence. Therefore, the "serving of <u>honor</u>," like that
of God, becomes mostly form. In fact, at times, it more
closely resembles the desire to save face than to maintain
genuinely admirable standards of conduct. For this reason
his gifted heroes constantly complain that "they must live

according to the notions of their neighbors." Manuel, the Count of Poictesme, feels that he had a geas, or obligation, to make a man of himself, imposed upon him by his mother,46 but no matter how hard he tries, he can not become the kind of person she wanted him to be. Wives, too, are good arbiters of conduct. Dame Lisa, Jurgen's wife, like a good Virginia lady, does not approve of Jurgen's clothes. His shirt, which had been given to him by Nessus, seems strange to her, and, besides, a button is missing.47 Since Cabell calls Jurgen's shirt his "genius," the author is probably also implying that Lisa is trying to stifle Jurgen's talent, just as Dejanira had killed her husband, Hercules, by giving him the poisoned shirt of the dying Centaur. That Cabell must have had this aspect of the myth in mind is further verified by the fact that Gisèle in The Silver Stallion wishes that her writer-husband's "silly dream-making would be taken away from . . . [him] so that . . . [they] might live in some sort of reputable and commonsense way."48

This somewhat misguided sense of honor, which, Cabell thought, could, at times, become downright harmful, was characteristic, not only of individuals, but of the whole of his society. In Townsend of Lichfield (1929), Cabell wrote that well-bred Virginians were wont to gloss over the misdemeanors of their own class. He said, ". . . we [and here he included himself, as he frequently did] had the rule of thumb . . . that 'immoral' conduct did not exist until some open mention of it was printed in the newspapers. . . ." Any "difficulty," he wrote, such as embezzlement, "was quietly settled out of court," and "nobody went to jail. The jail was for colored people. . . ."49 It was this pride of race and of clan that forced the Virginians to compensate for the disastrous events of the War by fabricating a past for themselves "in the more freely interpretative form of fiction." Cabell's own "Biography" is, in fact, a vast parody of Virginia's "superb and philanthropic romanticizing of history," for it is a fictitious history of the First Families of Lichfield (i.e., Richmond).

Perhaps one of the clearest expositions of the Virginian's "polite formula for exorcising the inadmissible,"50 is in Something About Eve. In this novel Gerald Musgrave wanders about for a time in Dreamland, where he is attracted to all sorts of beautiful damsels, while the Sylan, Glaum-Without-Bones, take his place in Lichfield. When Gerald returns home, he finds that, to all appearances, he has remained faithful to one woman after all. His fidelity is a rather dubious virtue, however, since this "one woman" is his mistress, rather than his wife, and she is his cousin, to boot, but then most of Virginia's "gentry" are distantly related, and so form a vast cousinage. When Gerald returns to Lichfield and finds that his reputation has been kept inviolate, he says complacently, "I have been kept in everything a model American citizen. I have gracefully adhered to the code of a gentleman. In my private life I have evinced every proper respect for the chivalrous sacrament of adultery between social equals. In the field of my professional labors I have composed no puerile and lascivious romances, but only serious and instructive works. I am, in brief, in all respects, a credit to my native Lichfield, and, more generally, to the United States of America."51

The final section of the triune system of ethics of the Virginia gentleman is his sense of obligation to his lady, which stems from domnei, the deification and consequent worship of women. In Cabell's books the heroes are presented with various types of maidens who seem ideal, for one reason or another. There are the youthful loves, such as Stella in The Cords of Vanity, who, in the "Poictesme" series, becomes Ettarre (an anagram for Retreat but also probably associated in Cabell's mind with the French word étoile, meaning star and the English word star, thereby making her the spiritual descendant of Stella, Latin for Star). Others among these youthful loves are Dorothy la Désirée in Jurgen and Evadne in Something About Eve. This type in Jurgen shades off into Helen, a symbol of unattainable perfection. Then, there are the women who represent purely physical love, such as Anaitis in Jurgen or Evasherah in Something About Eve. Next, there is intellectual love, represented by Marian Winwood in The Cords of Vanity and Evaine in Something About Eve.

Although all of these women, when viewed from afar, seem to the heroes to be beautiful, unattainable goddesses, upon closer acquaintance, they invariably turn out to be like the mothers who had produced them. They nag and scold and talk incessantly. They are certain that they are all wise, such as Evaine, the learned "fox-spirit" in Something About Eve, who worships all gods and is informed upon every subject, from the original habitat of the wild Bankiva fowl, through the complete list of the Seven Wonders of the World, to the main events in Milton's life and his principal works. What is worse, she divests herself of this erudition in the veriest clichés.52

Most of the maidens, if brought home, in some way or

another, reduce their husband's genius. Just as Dame Lisa in Jurgen and Gisele in The Silver Stallion both resent their husband's "dream-making" and wish that this "gift" would be taken away from him, so Evasherah and Evaine want an honorarium in return for their favors--Gerald's horse, Kalki, a Pegasus surrogate. Even Maya in Something About Eve, the most satisfactory of Cabell's women, saps at her husband's self-confidence by her low opinion of him. Gerald, the hero, likes to think of himself as the "Fair-haired Hoo, the Helper and Preserver, the Lord of the Third Truth, the well-beloved of Heavenly Ones."[53] When the inevitable visiting bishop comes to the home of this pair on Mispec Moor, Maya speaks disparagingly of Gerald, saying that he thinks he is a god. "He believes," she says that "he is the fair-haired Hoodoo, the Yelper and the Pretender, or something of that sort."[54] As a result, marriage and art seem so incompatible that in The Silver Stallion the writer Miramon Lluagor declares that "the marriage-bed is the grave of art," and wishes his wife into the middle of next week,[55] but then he misses her and wishes her back again, even though he knows that his chances for the creation of beautiful "designs" (books) will be somewhat limited by her presence.[56] Usually, the heroes, though nagged at endlessly by their wives, do want to continue living with them, for they know that the reality can never approach the ideal, and, after all, the earthly wives do love their husbands, cook and sew for them, and give them their children. Maya miraculously produces for Gerald his beloved son, Theodorick Quentin Musgrave, the only person to whom he is willing to relinquish Kalki.

Domnei, then, like the belief in God and in honor, is exposed as being merely another attempt on the part of the well-born Virginian to create "what ought to be" rather than to accept "what is."

If human ideas have no basis in fact, what, then, should be the attitude of the individual who rejects the illusions of his society? This is a question which Cabell asked himself constantly. In The Silver Stallion he set forth the various ways of reacting toward the myths of one's people, in the effort to find the best way of adjusting to them.

In the beginning of this novel, Horvendile, who seems to have replaced Charteris as Cabell's alter ego, sends seven of the nine followers of Manuel on their last "siege."[57] The object of the quest of each of the seven knights is to find the answer to Cabell's dilemma.[58]

The first knight is dispatched to the "fundamentalist

South," where, like Cabell in The Rivet in Grandfather's Neck, he tells the truth and has his head cut off. The second hero goes to the North, where he writes in his Ivory Tower, much as Cabell had done, and ignores the myth. The third goes to the West to bring back Manuel to dispel the myth, but he is told by the "redeemer" to keep the myth; the belief alone will miraculously make men braver, wiser, and better than they might otherwise be. The fourth knight travels to the East in search of wisdom; but he submits to pressure and becomes the weak, flabby Sylan, Glaum-Without-Bones, who accepts the myth--as do most people--although it does not make much sense to him. The fifth goes "underground," where he searches for the truth in books, only to come to the conclusion, which he had known subconsciously from the start, that "life is a pageant that passes very quickly, going hastily from one darkness to another with only ignes fatui to guide; and there is no sense in it."59 The sixth is a hypocrite; he stays in Poictesme (Virginia) and pretends to accept the myth, while, actually, he does all that he can to undermine it. The seventh accepts the myth wholeheartedly and continues to believe in it, even though he ironically destroys the belief in Manuel by himself becoming the Man-God in the worlds of his own creation. Somehow man is improved by his illusions, even though they have no basis in fact. In this last episode, as well as in Manuel's advice to Coth, the third knight, Cabell is but reiterating the rather startling conclusion to which he had come at the end of Beyond Life: Even though there may be no truth whatsoever in man's illusions, his myths, and his romances, they are so potent a force, they so "visibly . . . sway all life," that they themselves may well be God.60

In fact, even if one only pretends to believe, he may be rewarded. Alianora in Figures of Earth knows the truth about a certain goose-feather, which is supposed to have "magical" properties, but because she has the good sense to keep quiet, she attains her goal.61 Cabell usually takes the position of Miramon Lluagor, the writer-knight in The Silver Stallion, that the best policy is to "keep mum with Manuel," although in actual life he could not always do so. At least, this course would perhaps earn for Miramon-Cabell, as it had for that "dull witted and shrewd 'fellow'" Manuel, an enviable reputation "for impenetrable wisdom and boundless resource."62

Poictesme was, then, a wonderful device by which Cabell could give the illusion of keeping silent. Poictesme was a great relief mechanism for him. Like Jurgen's "cantrap,"63 it provided him with the magic formula by which he could enter the Heaven of his dreams from the Hell of actuality.

After having finished the "Biography of the Life of Manuel," Cabell seems to have felt that his magnum opus had been completed. At least, he truncated his name to "Branch Cabell," probably to suggest that the most individual part of himself had been sloughed off and that he was returning to his fathers, the Branches and the Cabells. Although he continued to criticize Virginia in his later books, he did not transform it to Poictesme. Perhaps the most amusing criticism which he launched against his neighbors in later years is in <u>Let Me Lie</u>, which, by the very double-entendre of its title, suggests both the reluctance of his native state to face the truth and its desire to be left to lie somnolent in its own dreams.

Cabell's translation of Virginia did, however, lift his work from the purely local and regional to the universal. In spite of the fact that the author was concerned primarily with the myth-making of Virginia, he saw that mankind, as a whole, must have illusions in order to exist. He knew, also, that these illusions do produce some admirable people, such as Jurgen's old grandmother, Steinvor. Poictesme afforded to the artist Cabell the proper artistic distance for writing about Virginia "humorously." Poictesme may, in fact, have provided Cabell with his immortality. Through his skillful blending of southern France and southern Virginia, he may, indeed, have reached Antan, that "land" of perfection so earnestly sought by his heroes.

NOTES

¹These tales were collected and published in The Line of Love (1905), Gallantry (1907), Chivalry (1909), and The Certain Hour (1916). The poetry appeared in a book entitled From the Hidden Way (1916). A romantic novel, The Soul of Melicent (later reissued as Domnei), was published in 1913.

²The three novels are The Eagle's Shadow (1904), The Cords of Vanity (1909), and The Rivet in Grandfather's Neck (1915). The short story is "The Lady of All Our Dreams," published in The Certain Hour (1916).

³Cabell, The Rivet in Grandfather's Neck, Works, XIV, 7.

⁴Ibid., p. 81.

⁵Ibid., p. 51.

⁶Ibid., p. 225.

⁷Cabell, "Another Note upon Lichfield," Townsend of Lichfield, Works, XVIII, 254-255.

⁸Cabell repeatedly intimated that he himself is in most of his heroes. See, for example, Quiet Please (Gainesville, Florida: University of Florida Press, 1952), pp. 8, 32, 63, 69, 104.

⁹Cabell, The Cords of Vanity, Works, XII, 165.

¹⁰Ibid., p. 135.

¹¹"A Note Upon Poictesme," Townsend of Lichfield, Works, XVIII, 239-241.

¹²William L. Godshalk, "James Branch Cabell at William and Mary: The Education of a Novelist," The William and Mary Review, V, No. 2 (Spring 1967), 3.

¹³Cabell, From the Hidden Way [and] The Jewel Merchants: Dizain and Comedy of Echoes, Works, XIII, 121-122.

¹⁴Cabell, Townsend of Lichfield, Works, XVIII, 241-242.

¹⁵Cabell, Let Me Lie, p. 283.

¹⁶Ibid., p. 134.

¹⁷Ibid.

¹⁸Ibid., p. 283.

¹⁹Ibid., pp. 145-146, 153-154.

[20] Cabell, "Precautional," Chivalry, Works, V, 5.
[21] Cabell, Let Me Lie, pp. 284-285.
[22] Ibid., pp. 168-169.
[23] Ibid., pp. 145, 172.
[24] Cabell, Townsend of Lichfield, Works, XVIII, 241.
[25] Cabell, Let Me Lie, p. 247. The major works in which Poictesme appears after The Cream of the Jest are Jurgen (1919), Figures of Earth (1921), The High Place (1923), Straws and Prayer-Books (1924), The Silver Stallion (1926), and Something About Eve (1927).
[26] Cabell, Straws and Prayer-Books, Works, XVII, xv.
[27] Cabell, Townsend of Lichfield, Works, XVIII, 239, 248.
[28] While William and Mary is not technically called a "university," in America, it would qualify in some respects for this designation, according to popular European concepts.
[29] Cabell, Let Me Lie, pp. 42, 262.
[30] Ibid., pp. 46-50.
[31] Cabell, Beyond Life, Works, I, 173-174.
[32] Ibid., p. x.
[33] Cabell, Jurgen, Works, VI, 255.
[34] Ibid., pp. 299-302.
[35] Ibid., pp. 260-262.
[36] Ibid., pp. 302-303.
[37] Ibid., p. 303.
[38] Cabell, The Silver Stallion, Works, III, 210-211.
[39] Cabell, Figures of Earth, Works, II, 288-289. Also, Cabell, The Silver Stallion, Works, III, 3-4.
[40] Cabell, The Silver Stallion, Works, III, 3-5.
[41] Ibid., p. 16.
[42] Cabell, The High Place, Works, VIII, 62-65.
[43] Ibid., pp. 256-257.
[44] Cabell, The Silver Stallion, Works, III, 19-20.
[45] Cabell, Jurgen, Works, VI, 304-305.

[46] Cabell, *Figures of Earth*, *Works*, II, 4.

[47] Cabell, *Jurgen*, *Works*, VI, 356.

[48] Cabell, *The Silver Stallion*, *Works*, III, 62.

[49] Cabell, *Townsend of Lichfield*, *Works*, XVIII, 20.

[50] Cabell, *Something About Eve: A Comedy of Fig-Leaves*, *Works*, X, 311.

[51] *Ibid.*

[52] *Ibid.*, pp. 115-120.

[53] *Ibid.*, e. g. pp. 121, 243.

[54] *Ibid.*, p. 251.

[55] Cabell, *The Silver Stallion*, *Works*, III, 67.

[56] *Ibid.*, pp. 74-75.

[57] *Ibid.*, pp. 8-14. The fates of two of the Fellowship, Anavalt and Holden, are dealt with in *Straws and Prayer-Books*, *Works*, XVII, 114-125, 206-214.

[58] See note 8.

[59] Cabell, *The Silver Stallion*, *Works*, III, 205.

[60] Cabell, *Beyond Life*, *Works*, I, 270.

[61] Cabell, *Figures of Earth*, *Works*, II, 64.

[62] Cabell, *The Silver Stallion*, *Works*, III, 56.

[63] Cabell, *Jurgen*, *Works*, VI, 292-295.

A CASE OF LITERARY PIRACY?

During his long lifetime James Branch Cabell was often accused by his critics of a lack of originality. In fact, on one occasion Richard Le Gallienne had gone so far as to dub him "a master of the pastiche," accusing him of masquerading in the ideas of such varied predecessors as Voltaire, Dumas, Heine, Stevenson, Wilde, and Hewlett.[1] Yet, in spite of the fact that critics thought that they had detected throughout Cabell's books numerous themes and turns of expression which had been used by others, only once was he actually accused by a living author of outright plagiarism.

Just after the publication of Cabell's <u>There Were Two Pirates</u> in 1946, E. D. Lambright, the editor of the <u>Tampa Tribune</u> at that time, said that Cabell had borrowed "liberally" from a "history" of Gasparilla[2] which Lambright had himself published in 1936 to justify Tampa's famed February fete in honor of western Florida's legendary pirate. Mr. Lambright offered as proof of Cabell's plagiarism the fact that the Richmond author had appropriated many of the "names and incidents" which Lambright had himself "invented" for his semi-authentic account of the pirate.[3]

A comparison of the two books reveals that Cabell had indeed borrowed "names," "incidents," and even complete characters from his predecessor. For example, from Lambright Cabell appropriated Gasparilla's colorful partner in crime, Roderigo Lopez, a figure who had not appeared in Lambright's printed sources.[4] From the Tampa editor Cabell filched the <u>Florida Blanca</u>, the ship upon which the two rapscallions had served in the Spanish Navy and in which they had made their escape in 1782 when Gasparilla had been accused of stealing jewels belonging to the Crown. Cabell followed his predecessor in calling a minor character <u>Sanibel</u>, after one of the islands in Charlotte Harbor, the refuge of the pirates from any possible pursuers.

Frequently, too, Cabell's events do resemble closely those of Lambright. In fact, they are sometimes expressed in similar terms. For example, Lambright's statement that when the pirates had landed upon Gasparilla Island, "they erected 12 houses of palmetto logs, thatched with palms strengthened with sturdier trees of the mainland,"[5] is followed closely by Cabell, who wrote, they "builded houses of palmetta logs, which . . . [they] thatched with palm leaves."[6]

Lambright's statement that "the older and less favored with good looks [among Gasparilla's women captives] were assigned as cooks, dishwashers, scrubwomen and laundresses,"[7] is but slightly altered by Cabell to become: "the elderly or the ugly I [Gasparilla] assigned to duty as our chambermaids, our laundresses, and our cooks."[8] Cabell did, then, follow Lambright a little too closely for the resemblances to be considered purely accidental.

In view of Cabell's obvious familiarity with Lambright's details, the Richmond author had to confess, when confronted with the accusation of plagiarism, that he had borrowed from Lambright's book, adding somewhat cryptically, "along with other sources," and offered by way of excuse for his "theft" his ignorance of the fact that Lambright's account was not authentic history.[9] Yet, Cabell must have known of the legendary nature of Gasparilla; at least, he could have been apprised of this fact by his good friend, A. J. Hanna, with whom he had collaborated on the history of the St. Johns River just four years before. He must have been aware that Lambright was doing (though somewhat more ineptly, to be sure) the very same thing which he himself had done in The First Gentleman of America. He was embellishing a few scanty facts of history (or of legend, in the case of Gasparilla) to create myth for the benefit and instruction of his contemporaries.

Cabell's willingness to lay himself open to a possible charge of plagiarism is especially perplexing for two reasons. First, he himself seemed to admit that his pilfering had not been really necessary when he offered to remove Lambright's "inventions" from his text, adding somewhat loftily, "in view of their complete unimportance so far as goes my romance."[10] Secondly, this apparently "unnecessary" plagiarism seems all the more incomprehensible in view of the fact that Cabell had always been supersensitive about this very matter. In the twenties he had written in Straws and Prayer-Books: "The production of articles as to my plagiarism and obscenities has, in my time, ranked as a national industry."[11] Again, in the same book, he had complained, "I was both knave and imbecile, whose 'mannered' writing was mere kleptomania."[12] In the later years of his life he still seemed to feel sensitive about this charge, although by then this particular resentment had grown to be but a small part of his overall despair at the current eclipse of his literary reputation. As late as 1952, in Quiet, Please, he wrote that others seemed to look upon him as a "pretentious lewd humbug," a "midnight assassin," a "no-doubt homosexual halfwit."[13]

In spite of his apparent irritability on the subject of his plagiarism, he himself seems to have given some foundation for the accusations of his detractors in a passage in <u>Quiet, Please</u>, in which he explained how he had achieved <u>that style of</u> his which critics had inconsistently deemed "inimitable" in almost the same breath in which they had accused him of parroting others. He wrote that, in order to achieve his unique style, he had "adapted and blended with one another--in varying proportions, self-consciously and pharmaceutically, with a meticulous preciseness--the literary manner and the phrasing and the sentence building of scores upon scores of authors, selecting always those two or three or perhaps yet more writers who for . . . [his] book's purpose seemed imitable."[14] These words constitute, on the surface, as explicit an admission of guilt as one is likely to find in print. And, yet, as always with Cabell, there is more to this matter than meets the eye. As usual, Cabell's work is permeated with irony and serpentine convolutions of thought, in which he seems to be bending back upon his own words in a most contradictory fashion.

There is a temptation to attribute Cabell's plagiarism, especially in <u>There Were Two Pirates</u>, to a lack of inventive power, a deficiency which might have been accentuated with the advance of age. Although this explanation might suffice, in part, to explain his appropriation of the symbols and turns of expression of others, yet it does not do full justice to Cabell's work.

The answer to the vexatious little puzzle of Cabell's seemingly unscrupulous raid upon Lambright, in particular, and upon others, in general, can be found, not so much in the parts of the history of Gasparilla which Cabell borrowed from Lambright as in what he did not borrow. Cabell himself furnished a clue to the mystery when he entitled his little book <u>There Were Two Pirates</u> and subtitled it <u>A Comedy of Division</u>.

The <u>division</u> in Cabell's story occurs in the character of Gasparilla himself, who, through the machinations of one Don Diego de Arredondo, journeys with his ill-gotten gains to St. Augustine, where he lives a life of probity, while his alter ego, the shadow of his later self, blusters about Tampa. Through this same Don Diego de Arredondo, the pirate, immediately upon his arrival in St. Augustine, is permitted, for a time, to return to his own childhood, adolescence, and young manhood to see "how it all began."

Although Cabell's St. Augustine Gasparilla had in his youth some of the characteristics possessed by Lambright's Tampa reprobate in his younger days, there were significant differences. In their youth the two buccaneers had resembled each other in that both had been likeable villains who had a way with the ladies. Both, when young, had been possessed of a singular degree of culture and refinement, which seemed inconsistent with their later depravity. Both had had to compromise with their youthful ideals and ambitions, which both had derived from their preoccupation with the Middle Ages, although they differed in the aspects of this tumultuous period which appealed to them. Lambright's Tampa Gasparilla had been attracted primarily by the daring exploits of the knights of old from having read "the inspiriting accounts of the devoted Crusaders, battling at the walls of Jerusalem" and had "frequently used the name of 'Richard Coeur de Lion' bombastically as his own."15 On the other hand, Cabell's St. Augustine pirate had amassed a tremendous knowledge of Provençal poets, such as Geoffrey Rudel, Raimbaut de Vaqueras, and Pierre Vidal, and had decided to become, after he had grown up, a Provençal poet--that is, if he did not become a saint, such as St. George of Cappadocia. They differed, too, in the ultimate fate which was in store for each. The St. Augustine Gasparilla, invented by Cabell, did not wrap an anchor chain about his middle and plunge to his death in the waters of Charlotte Harbor, as had his Tampa counterpart, when beset with the United States Navy. Instead, he continued to live in St. Augustine in a state of uneasy affection with his wife, Isabel, until his death, presumably of natural causes, in 1828.

It is due to these significant changes in the lives and interests of the two pirates that it becomes apparent that, especially in the second half of Cabell's little romance, the author of There Were Two Pirates has left the world of Lambright's Tampa Gasparilla and has passed over, by dint of Don Diego's magic green stone, into the life of the "literary pirate," Mr. Cabell of Richmond-in-Virginia. This suspicion is confirmed by the fact that Cabell gives the character through whose magic this transformation is effected the name Diego, which, significantly enough, does mean James in English, while Arredondo suggests dryness, aridity.

Cabell, then, is only doing what he had done many times before; he is once again writing a highly universalized story of his own life. By giving his idealistic youth the criminal adult career of Gasparilla, King of the Pirates, he is ironically living "according to the notions of his neighbors," in fiction, if not in life. He is giving people the material for believing of him what they wanted to believe, even though, as Cabell maintained throughout his multi-volumed "Biography of the Life of Manuel," their beliefs may not necessarily accord with the facts.

For years, in his many novels and essays, Cabell had shown his preoccupation with the relationship between fact and fancy and had come to the conclusion that there is no very clear line of demarcation between the two. He must have felt that just as his critics were, to his way of thinking, often in error concerning the facts of his own life and letters, so they were probably mistaken about the corporate life of the race, in which religious beliefs have always played a major role.

As a result of this view, even in the first part of <u>There Were Two Pirates</u>, the section for which Cabell had borrowed from Lambright the most copiously, there are telling deviations from the original, for Cabell provided his rollicking little tale of the pirate with curious "religious" overtones. For example, Cabell's Gasparilla was born <u>not</u> in Barcelona, as Lambright would have it, but in the nearby Spanish town of Montserrat, the site of a great Benedictine monastery. The priest who performed marriage ceremonies between the pirates and their fair women captives had <u>not</u> been taken upon one of Gasparilla's raids, as he had in the chronicle according to Lambright, but he had been a willing participant in the original revolt of Gasparilla and Lopez against the captain of the <u>Floridablanca</u>. The mutiny of the three leaders of the conspiracy had taken place not merely in the latter part of 1783, as Lambright had written, but rather on the festival of the Conversion of St. Paul. The coast of Florida had been sighted, not in April of 1784, but rather on the Feast Day of St. Mary the Egyptian. In short, Cabell purposely provided his book with a religious orientation, which might seem inharmonious in this particular context, but which is standard procedure with Cabell.

These seemingly random religious touches reveal an aspect of Cabell's overall philosophy of life, which, in its turn, throws light upon his otherwise perplexing imitation of the words and ideas of others. Cabell's incongruous juxtaposition of the details of the pirate's criminal career with evidences of a profound religious faith shows Cabell's belief that the relationship between a man's morality and his religion is tenuous, to say the least. So far as Cabell could see, religion is simply a vast, cosmic Cinderella tale which enables a man to ease his way through life into what he hopes will be a state of bliss after death. Religion performs this valuable function for humans, whether its tenets be true or not. For the purpose for which it is intended, therefore, one faith might do as well as the next. In fact, even he, James Branch Cabell, might well create his own gospel, which he strongly suspected would be as efficacious as any other. And that is exactly what he did do. He isolated the features common to all religions--those concepts which Jung has made famous as archetypes--and imitated them in his own scripture, the "Biography of the Life of Manuel," an eighteen-volume chronicle of a rogue-redeemer who rode off to the West. Even though the tale of the departure of the dubious "hero" was fabricated originally by a small child to keep himself from being punished for coming in late, yet it was believed and perpetuated, and took on all the force of truth.

Cabell did borrow from his predecessors, but he was not merely aping irresponsibly the ideas and phrases which others had expressed from Homer to Joyce. He was a writer who was sophisticated enough to know that authors have constantly made use of the work of their predecessors. He knew, too, that the test of originality lies not so much in <u>what</u> a person writes as in <u>how</u> he writes it. Material, to be fresh, must be fired with the writer's own purpose and suffused with his own being. Cabell, then, used the archetypal image with a far different intent from that of most of his predecessors; when he used it, he did so to satirize the whole fabric of western civilization. The "Biography of the Life of Manuel" is, in fact, a vast parody of human beliefs, ideas, and hopes, which few people have understood, for, like most other "scriptures," the parts are usually read in isolation from each other.

Cabell must have been alternately maddened and amused by the lack of discernment of his critics. Only a few-- such as Carl Van Doren and Mencken in Cabell's heyday and, later, Edmund Wilson--penetrated his little arabesques.

When Cabell began going to Florida in 1935, he must have learned very soon of the Gasparilla festival. Because of his remarkable capacity for detecting the affinities in human phenomena, he was probably intrigued with the observance for the very reason that it constituted in itself a prime example of the ritualistic reincarnation of

an old myth. Moreover, when he had read Lambright's
explanation of the origin of the celebration, he must
have been struck immediately with the similarities not
only between his own writing techniques and those of
Lambright, but also between the actual life of the pirate
and that of James Branch Cabell, or, at least, with the
similarity of the impressions which each had made upon
his peers. Whether justly or unjustly, both were considered pirates, though in different media.

And, then, a daring idea must have entered Cabell's
mind. Why not do what his critics had always said that
he had done? Why not plagiarize this little known book?
Why not play a huge joke on those colossal idiots, his
critics, who had accused him of plagiarizing when he had
only been making use of that which writers had, from
time immemorial, considered public domain? He was quite
sure that "those Shining Ones," as he called his critics,
who knew so much more about writing than he did, would
not be perceptive enough to recognize a real, bona fide
case of plagiarism when they saw one. And as to the
people of Tampa? Well, with Cabell's idée fixe that
Southerners never read books anyway, he must have felt
that he was quite safe in that quarter. Besides, even
if they did read his book and accuse him of pilfering
from Lambright, the situation would be no different
from what it had been for years. What a delicious edge
would be given to his little joke, too, not only by
pirating the story of a pirate, but by simultaneously
spiriting Tampa's precious pirate from the West Coast
to St. Augustine, where Cabell made his winter home!

Needless to say, he was immensely successful with
his little ruse. Not one of his critics really guessed
what he was about. They wrote their usual nonsense
about his "style" and blamed his book either for being
or for not being another Jurgen. Orville Prescott wrote
in the pages of the Yale Review exactly what Cabell could
probably have predicted. He said of There Were Two
Pirates that "its magical fantasy and its suavely urbane
prose are exactly of the same variety as Mr. Cabell has
been producing for forty years," and closed with the
words, "slight and insubstantial as it is, this tedious
little tale seems padded to unnecessary length."[16]

Only one critic remotely skirted upon the truth.
Armistead Gordon, an English professor at the University
of Virginia, who was, by virtue of his Virginia
"nationality" and his profession, perhaps somewhat more
qualified than others to fathom Cabell's intricate
thought patterns, suggested that there might be more

pirates in Cabell's book than meet the eye. He referred to Cabell in a review which he wrote for the New York Times as the "triune" Cabell and even suggested that it might be possible to find four pirates in Cabell's little tale.[17] He did not accuse Cabell of any specific plagiarism, however, for he did not seem to know of the existence of Lambright's book.

Cabell's little joke did have its repercussions, however, as did many of his literary pleasantries. Although the people of Tampa probably had not read Cabell's book, they did read Armistead Gordon's review in the New York Times, in which the author unwittingly insulted the west Floridians when he assumed that Gasparilla had originally been a "resident of St. Augustine," but had "of recent years" been "seized upon as a patron saint by the Tampa Chamber of Commerce and Better Business Bureau."[18] Incensed at Gordon's assumption that they, the people of Tampa, had nefariously filched their beloved pirate from their rival city, they "erupted with a night letter"[19] to St. Augustine, in which they laid claim to their hero in no uncertain terms. They wrote:

> DEMONSTRABLY GASPARILLA NEVER RESIDENT REPUTEDLY OR OTHERWISE OF ST. AUGUSTINE. AFFIRMATIVE EVIDENCE THAT OLD FREE-BOOTER NEVER SET FOOT FLORIDA EAST COAST. GASPARILLA BELONGS IF NOT TO THE AGES AT LEAST TO TAMPA AND SOUTH-WEST FLORIDA WHERE RECORDED HISTORY AND LOCAL LEGEND ESTABLISH HIM AS NO JOHNNY COME LATELY.[20]

To this St. Augustine replied, "with a shade of austere dignity," according to the Richmond Times Dispatch:

> ST. AUGUSTINE WANTS NO CLAIM TO SECOND-RATE GASPARILLA. SIR FRANCIS DRAKE AND OTHERS ARE ALL WE CAN HANDLE IN OUR 381-YEAR-OLD HISTORY WHICH IS OVERCROWDED WITH CUT-THROATS.[21]

In his ironical and oblique fashion Cabell provided, perhaps, his own commentary on this amusing little controversy and others of the same ilk when he wrote in Quiet, Please concerning his self-confessed plagiarisms:

> And nobody ever caught me at these nefarious, so multiform alchemies; or, at least, nobody of large prominence has been at pains to expose me. [This, perhaps, is his way of getting back at such critics as Richard Le Gallienne, Armistead Gordon, and the city of Tampa.] The majority of virtuosi

have continued to print commentaries . . . upon that staple commodity, my "style," which, developing with <u>The Eagle's Shadow</u> in 1904, has prevailed steadfastly and unchanged through some fifty books, yes, even down to <u>The Devil's Own Dear Son</u> in 1949, so should I infer.22

And so, once more, this irrepressible literary prankster played one of his little practical jokes on humanity in order to ridicule the unreliability and repetitiveness of human thought and, as he said in <u>Quiet, Please</u>, to "half-drug and content . . . [him], selfishly, in a cloistered privateness."23

He laughed that he might not weep, but his laughter, like that of Penelope's suitors, threatened to change at any moment to blood and tears. The Richmond necromancer, in the midst of his parodying of the foibles of mankind, was keenly aware that he, too, as a member of the human species, was destined to share the human condition and so was subject to the general human fate. He knew far too well, as he wrote in his little allegory, "The Journey," that he and his works, along with all other human creatures and their toys, were destined to be swept "pell-mell into the dim incoherency, everywhere a-glitter with their scattered tinsels."24 He knew that, in spite of all man's efforts to avert annihilation, Death was the great thief of all human life and of all human endeavour. Death would inevitably have the last word, for this grim destroyer was the pirate <u>sans pareil</u>.

NOTES

[1]Richard Le Gallienne, "James Branch Cabell, Master of the Pastiche," New York Times, February 3, 1921, p. 3.

[2]Edwin Dart Lambright, The Life and Exploits of Gasparilla, Last of the Buccaneers, With the History of Ye Mystic Krewe of Gasparilla (Tampa, Florida: Millsboro Printing Company, 1936).

[3]"A Case of Lifting," Richmond Times-Dispatch, September 5, 1946, a report of an article by John N. Hutchins, entitled "East Coast-West Coast--and Mr. Cabell." New York Times Sunday Book Review, September 1, 1946, p. 10.

[4]Sources cited by Lambright on the reverse side of the title page of The Life and Exploits of Gasparilla.

[a]An American in Madrid who wished his name withheld.

[b]Bradlee, Francis B. C. Piracy in the West Indies and Its Suppression. Massachusetts: [The Essex Institute], 1923.

[c]Finger, Charles J. [No title is mentioned, but Finger did write a book called Great Pirates (Girard, Kansas: Haldeman-Julius Co., 1924).]

[d]Garnett, Burt P. Editorial Research Reports. [No other information is provided.]

[e]Gosse, Phillip. The Pirate Who's Who. London: Dulau and Company, Ltd., 1924.

[f]Reynolds, F[rancis] J[oseph]. Director of the P. F. Collier & Son Readers' Cooperative Service Bureau. [No other information is given, but he did write The United States Navy from the Revolution to Date (New York: P. F. Collier & Son, 1915).]

[g]Wilkinson, Warren H. Fort Myers. [No other information is given.]

[5]Lambright, The Life and Exploits of Gasparilla, p. 23.

[6]James Branch Cabell, There Were Two Pirates (New York: Farrar, Straus and Company, Inc., 1946), p. 17.

[7]Lambright, The Life and Exploits of Gasparilla, p. 25.

[8]Cabell, There Were Two Pirates, p. 23.

[9]Richmond Times-Dispatch, September 5, 1946.

[10]Ibid.

[11]Cabell, Straws and Prayer-Books, Works, XVII, p. 264.

[12]Ibid., p. 273.

[13] James Branch Cabell, *Quiet, Please*, p. 13.

[14] *Ibid.*, p. 47.

[15] Lambright, *The Life and Exploits of Gasparilla*, p. 8.

[16] Orville Prescott, "Outstanding Novels," *Yale Review*, XXXVI (Autumn, 1946), 189.

[17] Armistead Gordon, "Mellow, Triune Cabell," *New York Times*, April 11, 1946, p. 5.

[18] *Ibid.*

[19] "A Case of Lifting," *Richmond Times-Dispatch*, September 5, 1946.

[20] *Ibid.*

[21] *Ibid.*

[22] Cabell, *Quiet, Please*, p. 47.

[23] *Ibid.*

[24] Cabell, "The Journey," *Richmond Times-Dispatch*, January 31, 1932, Section III, Part 2, p. 2.

CABELL'S COMIC MASK

It has become quite the fashion among recent Cabell critics to emphasize the comic elements in Cabell's artistic vision at the expense of the tragic features which are present, too, throughout much of his writing. In fact, Cabell's comic mask served through most of his career to hide the deep sense of tragedy which lay at the heart of much of his work.

Arvin R. Wells gave guarded expression to almost this same idea when he wrote on the last page of his study, <u>Jesting Moses: A Study of Cabellian Humor</u> (1962), that "like all seriously intended comedy, Cabellian comedy may be said to rejoice over the endless fertility of life. . . ." Then he added, "It approaches tragedy in its attempt to transcend the whole of the finite predicament (for Cabell, the naturalistic dilemma) and thereby to reconcile man to his role in the scheme of things."[1] In actuality, though, Cabell's thought did more than merely "approach" tragedy. Throughout much of his life his philosophical outlook was essentially tragic.

What has puzzled critics has been partly the wit, humor, and persiflage which accompany Cabell's gloomy meditations on the fate of man and partly his habit of terming many of the works which make up the "Biography of the Life of Manuel" "comedies." For example, he subtitled <u>The Eagle's Shadow</u> "A Comedy of Purse-Strings"; <u>The Rivet in Grandfather's Neck</u>, "A Comedy of Limitations"; <u>The Cream of the Jest</u> and <u>The Lineage of Lichfield</u>, "Two Comedies of Evasion"; <u>The Silver Stallion</u>, "A Comedy of Redemption." Readers naturally assume that if Cabell said that his works are comedies, they must be so. Cabell's words, however, must never be taken too literally, for his remarks are usually clothed in irony, sometimes of a most subtle and elusive variety; in fact, he is rather likely to mean exactly the opposite of what he says.

Most of Cabell's literary inspiration seems to have come from what he had read in his youth--up until his graduation from William and Mary. Since he had specialized in French, it is from the French, together with the older English and German writers, that he derived his conception of comedy. To the student of French literature, and particularly of older French literature, in which Cabell was deeply interested, a comedy does not necessarily mean a comedy at all, in the usual sense of the term.[2] It means simply a play of any kind; in fact, it can be tragic. In France a comédien is not necessarily a comedian, but he can be an actor of any type. On the stage of the Comédie française tragedies are more likely to be presented than comedies.

Cabell, then, is, in general, using the word comedy to mean simply an action which imitates "reality," in much the same way as Shakespeare had thought of human activities in his famous lines in As You Like It, which begin:

>All the world's a stage,
>And all the men and women merely players.
>They have their exits and their entrances;
>And one man in his time plays many parts,
>His acts being seven ages. . . .[3]

Throughout much of Cabell's literary life the sense of tragedy which besets the individual was usually present beneath the surface banter. One of the earliest notes of disenchantment was sounded in his little poem, "The Castle of Content," written when Cabell was only sixteen. The sense of the evanescence of the particular, which was to haunt Cabell throughout much of his life, is already present in such lines as the following:

>The towers are fallen; no laughter rings
>Through the rafters, charred and rent;
>The ruin is wrought of all goodly things
>In the Castle of Content.[4]

Just what occurrence had precipitated this poem is difficult to say. There may, in fact, have been no specific event, but simply the coming of age of an adolescent--the realization that life is not all that it seems. The theme of the reconciliation of appearance and actuality has been one which has captivated the world since Adam and Eve first ate the fruit of the tree of the knowledge of good and evil in the Garden of Eden.

When a man becomes cognizant of the ugly realities of life, he must, of necessity, try to minimize them by glossing them over, both for his own sake and for the sake of others. This maintenance of the proper outward show by the assumption of a mask is closely allied with Cabell's theory of comedy; in fact, it is one of its sources. For this reason Cabell returned again and again to the theme of "appearances." For example, in 1921, he labeled Figures of Earth "A Comedy of Appearances." In this work Manuel says several times that his mother had given him a geas, which is the obligation to make a man of himself and to maintain a good front before the world.5 In view of the fact that in The High Place (1923) Cabell was to make much of a gander--a male goose--who was forever singing platitudes, he may have meant the pronunciation of the word geas to resemble geese.6 Although critics have found other meanings in this word geas, he may have meant really that Manuel's mother had wanted him to make an ass of himself by following the precepts of the herd or flock, like the other geese of the world. This hypothesis is supported by the fact that the dominating symbol of Figures of Earth is a goose feather, to which foolish man attributes miraculous properties because they believe that it is a feather from the Zhar-Ptitza bird.7

    The theme of appearances occurs again in Jurgen when Dame Lisa reproaches the hero because a button of his shirt is missing. It is implicit in the passage in Something about Eve when Gerald Musgrave congratulates himself for having "adhered to the code of a gentleman,"8 in appearance, at least, even though he had actually been derelict in his duties in this world. It was this compulsion which led Cabell, the artist, to mask frequently his pessimism concerning the nature and the fate of man with a badinage which he did not actually feel.

    Likewise, it was this same compulsion which led Cabell in real life to present to the world--the reporters, the admiring fans, the scholars, and the budding writers who came to his door--an air of geniality, of urbanity, and of unfailing courtesy, which he did not always feel, judging from his outbursts in Special Delivery, a volume of the letters which Cabell would like to have written to his correspondents. Cabell was, after all, a Virginia gentleman, and it is difficult for other Americans to realize the rather strict social code which still prevails in the section of Virginia extending for some one hundred and fifty miles around the city of Richmond. There is here a note of decorum which stems from eighteenth-century England. A Virginia gentleman or lady simply must not "wear his heart on his sleeve," to use an old cliché. There is much attention accorded to correct demeanor and to the preservation of the even tenor of life. The arts are somewhat suspect in this area, for they are likely to lead to immoderate application, at the least, and, consequently, they take people away from their proper métier in life--that of extending and receiving hospitality. They make a person "tacky," a term which in Virginia refers to slovenliness, not only in dress, but in behavior as well.

Through the middle years of his life, Cabell, like all other people, was forced to adjust himself to a world which was not exactly what his youthful dreams had led him to expect. First, there was the dichotomy in his life style, which was demanded, on the one hand, by the society in which he lived and, on the other, by his desire to attain perfection in his art. This schism must have been increased by his marriage to a proper Virginia lady with five children. The adjustment must have been difficult on both sides, for Cabell was already a bachelor of thirty-four, who, by his own admission, had been somewhat spoiled, first, by his nurse, Miss Louisa Nelson,[9] and, then, it may be conjectured, by the limited adulation which had accompanied his first books. He had been accustomed, in short, to having his own way. Virginia ladies insist that all who may chance to fall within their jurisdiction must keep up appearances at all costs. As Cabell said so many times, their charges must do what is expected of them. The clash in life patterns must have required much adjustment on both sides.

The situation was not helped much by the unfavorable reception which attended most of his books through the middle period of his life. For the most part, they fell, both at home and abroad, upon a world which remained relatively unimpressed. Cabell once wrote sadly, ". . . the persons about whom I really care will never read whatever I may elect to publish, nor ever, if by unforseeable circumstances compelled to read me, could they take my nonsense seriously."[10] This neglect is a bitter truth, of course, which almost all writers have had to face from time immemorial. He was mystified, too, by the fact that even as early as The Eagle's Shadow the world at large greeted each of his books with, as he put it, "incoherent rage" and "unexplained fury."[11] This sort of continued denunciation can be damaging to the morale of the most hardy artisan, but, to a sensitive artist, it must have been devastating. His state of mind could not have been improved much by the hue and cry surrounding Jurgen. Although the indictment of the book did make his name known far and wide, his fame had come to him, in his estimation, for the wrong reasons.

By the time that he was writing Straws and Prayer-Books, which was published in 1924, and The Silver Stallion, which was brought out in 1925, Cabell had come to feel that life for the individual is a poor affair, for, on this earth, it is a Walburga's Eve, as he called it again and again, and, after death, there does not seem to be much to hope for either, as he had indicated in his account of Jurgen's visit to Heaven. In the twenties, then, he seems to have reached the nadir of his depression. In fact, the very title of the first of these two works, <u>Straws and Prayer-Books</u>, is indicative of the mood in which the book was written, for the essays within it are concerned with the theme expressed by the lines of Alexander Pope in <u>An Essay on Man</u>--that man in his despair will snatch at anything, a straw or a prayer-book, to prevent him from thinking too much about the human predicament. Pope had written:

> Behold the child, by Nature's kindly law,
> Pleased with a rattle, tickled with a straw;
> Some lovely plaything gives his youth delight,
> A little louder, but as empty quite:
> Scarfs, garters, gold, amuse his riper stage,
> And beads, and prayer-books are the toys of age.
> Pleased with this bauble still, as that before,
> Till tired he sleeps, and life's poor play is o'er.[12]

These lines, which are quoted in part by Cabell on one of the opening unnumbered pages of the book, serve to reinforce his conviction that life, at best, is but a "poor play." In <u>The Silver Stallion</u> he expressed again the same idea when he wrote that "life is a pageant that passes very quickly, going hastily from one darkness to another with only ignes fatui to guide; and there is no sense in it."[13] Certainly, through the books of this period the word <u>comedy</u> does not mean <u>comedy</u> in the usual sense of the term.

Through these years, Cabell saw life as a gloomy corridor which was dark at both ends, an image which, with some minor alterations, he may have borrowed, perhaps unconsciously, from Flaubert's <u>Madame Bovary</u>, in which the main character, Emma Bovary, looks upon "the future . . . [as] a long, dark corridor with its door at the end shut fast."[14] In <u>Straws and Prayer-Books</u>, in the chapter headed "Romantics about Them," he wrote, "There is always ahead, and always a little nearer, the one and one only exit from the familiar corridor of our workaday existence. All of us thus pass, futilely, nesciently, and helplessly, through tedium to horror: for we live <u>in articulo mortis;</u> our doings here, when unaffectedly regarded, are but the restlessness of a prolonged demise; and the birth cry of every infant announces the beginning of the death agony . . . ."15 At this point Cabell breaks off with four spaced periods, a device which he frequently used when contemplating the subject of death, as though he were drawing back with the same horror at the inevitable conclusion of life as that experienced by the generality of men. Again, a few pages later on, he wrote: ". . . death is the one impending fact which is certain. Now, when thought of in its physical aspects, death is an indignity before which any sort of human self-respect . . . becomes preposterous. Thought about logically, it makes any conceivable human action rather silly, as upon the whole inappropriate to condemned persons in a death-cell."16 Cabell's attitude to death is, in fact, strongly reminiscent of one of Pascal's *Pensées*, in which the latter had written:

> Let us imagine a number of men in chains, and all condemned to death, where some are killed each day in the sight of the others, and those who remain see their own fate in that of their fellows, and wait their turn, looking at each other sorrowfully and without hope. It is an image of the condition of men.17

Cabell, however, is much more realistic than Pascal in his reaction to man's fate when he remarks: "And so beyond doubt the majority of us act wiseliest by not thinking about it at all, except as a regrettable accident which happens to other people."18 As Cabell had written in the introduction to *Straws and Prayer-Books*, man retains "forever inviolate that frigid, and pale, and hard, small core of selfishness which" is "the heart of Manuel."19

Although Cabell had always at the center of his philosophy this sense of impending doom, yet, like Kerin and Kerin's wife, Saraïde, in *The Silver Stallion*, and like people everywhere, for that matter, he had decided, evidently, that man should make the best of a bad situation and find what solace he can from creature comforts. For this reason, when Kerin returns home from his diligent search after "the Truth," Cabell has the husband and wife go "silently, from the twilight into the darkness of the house which" they had shared since their youth, and Saraïde (of the eternal tribe of Sarah) lights a fire, somewhat irreverently, with Kerin's bit of paper upon which he had written the truth, which he had garnered from years of "long endeavor." When the pair are basking in their eight-sided home, which has become snug and warm and cozy looking--eight, a box for two, which would eventually be replaced by two grim, four-sided boxes, one for each--

Kerin decides that "it could benefit nobody ever to recognize--either in youth or in gray age or after death,--that time, like an old, envious eunuch, must endlessly deface and maim, and make an end of, whatever anywhere was young and strong and beautiful or even cozy. . . ." (These spaced periods are not Cabell's.) "Saraïde . . . [likewise] seemed to have found out for herself, somewhere in philanthropic fields, the one thing which was wholly true; and she seemed, also, to prefer to ignore it, in favor of life's unimportant, superficial, familiar tasks. . . ."[20] Again, he used those disquieting four spaced periods.

Kerin and Saraïde's little home was but one of those "colorful alcoves" in which the individual might dally for a time in his course through life and about which Cabell had written in the first chapter of <u>Straws and Prayer-Books</u>. These recesses may range from "surrender to the invigorating lunacy of herd action," he says, to "mental concentration upon new dance-steps and the problems of chess and auction bridge." "Indeed," Cabell says, one may blunder "into a rather handsome number of such alcoves which . . . temporarily shut out . . . the only exit of the inescapable corridor." By this means, he concludes, ". . . life's monotonous main tenor is thus diversified by an endless series of slight distracting interests and of small but very often positive pleasures in the way of time-wasting and of misdemeanor. And, in addition, as we go, all sorts of merry tales are being interchanged, about what lies beyond the nearing door and the undertaker's little black bag."[21]

Cabell, then, looks, upon all that humans do--including the writing and reading of novels--as means for the "perennation of optimism" so "that nobody really needs to notice how the most of us, in unimportant fact, approach toward death through gray and monotonous corridors."[22] He wrote that "everywhere that creating romantic who lives in every human being is composing or else borrowing the kind of romance which most potently diverts him, and prevents his going mad."[23] The diversion of the writer, then, seems to vary only in extent and in effectiveness from that of humanity at large. Like Schiller, Cabell wrote in his first lines of "A Note on Alcoves" that "the literary artist plays: and the sole end of his endeavor is to divert himself. . . ."[24] Then Cabell went on to say that for nearly a quarter of a century he had been toying with the "Biography of the Life of Manuel" to divert himself. Even as late as 1952, in <u>Quiet, Please</u>, he wrote that he had been engaging in his "nefarious, so multiform alchemies," which, he explained, is his careful blending of "the literary manner and the phrasing and the sentence building of scores upon scores of authors . . . to the sole end that these piddling labors should half-drug and content . . . [him], selfishly, in a cloistered privateness."25 When Cabell wrote in that fashion upon his own so-called "borrowing," he was simply making an amused and ironical comment upon the inconsistency of critics who leveled the accusation of plagiarism at him in the same breath in which they remarked upon his distinctive style. Although he says that he had enjoyed every moment of this "time-wasting," upon the "Biography," yet six years before his death he still retained a remnant of the theme which had occupied so much of his thinking in the middle part of his life--that man has to engage in little pastimes to prevent him from thinking about the one truth which is inescapably certain.

Admittedly, there are notes of optimism scattered throughout Cabell's works. Most noticeable is the wit and sardonic humour which pervade his books. Much of the time, however, he is laughing not so much <u>with</u> the human race as <u>at</u> it for its posturing, its romances, and its evasions of the truth. Fortunately, however, and especially as he grew older, he included himself in this Gargantuan laughter. In fact, in <u>The Silver Stallion</u> the man Donander, who becomes a god in the universes which he creates, is but Cabell himself in the worlds of his own creation, for, by this time, he, like Donander, had become something of a myth. The very work <u>Donander</u> is probably a blend of <u>Don</u> (Sir) with gander, the male "goose," who, in <u>The High Place</u> was ever sagely singing in his hut in Upper Morven, just as Cabell was forever writing in his study on the second floor of his home on Monument Avenue in Richmond-in-Virginia, and, probably much like Cabell himself, Milord Gander hated to be interrupted when he was "composing." The purpose of this deathless gander, like that of all who seek to inspire humanity, "is to fill . . . [his] fellows with a sentiment of their importance as moral beings and of the greatness of their destinies." Florian, the hero of this book, noticed that "the aesthetic theories of this insane bird coincided rather oddly with St. Hoprig's theories. . . ."26 In other words, all humanity--geese, saints, writers alike--is busily deceiving itself. "Mundus vult decipi,"27 Cabell had said, was the motto of Manuel, for Cabell had come to the conclusion that man's very dullness, vanity, and stupidity force him to weave romances which do incredibly bring about a better world. He wrote in <u>Beyond Life</u> "that the accepted routine of life's conduct tends to make mountebanks of us inevitably: and the laborious years weave small hypocrisies like cobwebs about our every action, and at last about our every thought. The one consoling feature is that we are so incessantly busied at concealment of our personal ignorance and incapacity as to lack time to detect one another. For we are all about that arduous task of doing what seems to be expected of us. A few lines later on, he says, "And not the least remarkable part of the astounding business is that this continuous pretending by everybody appears to answer fairly well. It passes the pragmatic test: it works, and upon the whole it works without bringing about intolerable disaster. . . ."[28] That is the colossal joke about human existence, and that is probably one of the reasons why he termed his work "comedies." This self-deception is "the cream of the jest." Even though, as he had John Charteris say in Beyond Life, "human ideas are probably not ever correct about anything. . . . . . [and] should be valued only as the playthings "which enable man "to forget, for a while at least, the darkness of Walburga's Eve which encompasses his present lodgings, everywhere, within such easy reaching distance."[29] This delusion is perhaps optimism, but an inverted optimism.

Moreover, there is a degree of optimism expressed again by John Charteris in Beyond Life, when he says "that we are components of an unfinished world, and that we are but as seething atoms which ferment toward its making, if merely because man as he now exists can hardly be the finished product of any Creator whom one could very heartily revere." "We are being made [Charteris thought] into something quite unpredictable . . . and we are sustained, through the purging and the smelting, by an instinctive knowledge that we are being made into something better." This view might be interpreted as being fairly optimistic, were it not that Cabell somewhat negates his contention by attributing the desire "to have the creatures of earth and the affairs of earth, not as they are, but 'as they ought to be'" to the will of man himself.[30] This desire seems to leave little room for the beneficent deity presiding over all. Once again, then, Cabell's optimism seems to be a matter of mere wishful thinking on the part of man himself. Much of the time Cabell apparently was of the opinion that even though the whole might possibly be tending toward something better, yet each individual must still live through his own personal Walburga's Eve and must face his own death and dissolution.

As Cabell grew older, however, he became much more willing to accept the possibility of the existence of a deity who might be presiding over the affairs of men, for he wrote in Quiet, Please, "--For about God, I find, I do not often think nowadays, either one way or another, except only with this constant but vague sense of gratitude for His past and present favors, in the event of His indeed being somewhere upstairs."31

Perhaps there is some divine dispensation which allows an individual to accept the probability of misfortune philosophically the nearer he comes to it. By his sixties and seventies, many of the earlier problems of Cabell's life had been resolved. His children had grown up and were largely on their own. He had a fine row of books to his credit. He had learned to accept his own literary eclipse, and, finally, he had gained something of a new lease on life when he had broken the Richmond syndrome by going to St. Augustine in the winters and to Poynton Lodge in the Northern Neck of Virginia in the summers. It is a tribute to Richmond, however, that when he and his wife were forced by their health to seek a warmer climate, they chose a town in the deep South as nearly like Richmond as they could find. This was the period in Cabell's life when he could write, ". . . I nowadays render heavenward my uncertain, tentative thanks for an as yet unimpaired liver; . . . for the beauty of moonlit nights; . . . for the possibilities of English prose; and for the elations of alcohol. . . ."32 It was in this mellow period of his life, the period in which the human animal attains to a remarkable degree of resignation in view of the imminence of death, that most of the younger critics now writing had probably known him. He had succeeded in convincing even himself that all is well, for in Lichfield and in Richmond, as in Poictesme, "Mundus vult decipi," and perhaps all really is well when one has completed the work which he has set out to do.

Although Cabell had called some eleven of his works "comedies," each nevertheless was a wry sort of comedy. He explained in "The Epistle Dedicatory" to The Lineage of Lichfield (1921) that he had adopted this comoedic metaphor, because "really there is thin sustenance for the tragic muse in the fact that with each performance the costume of the protagonist is spoiled, and the human body . . . is thrown perforce to the dust-heap," since, as he goes on to say, with each generation the human spirit clothes itself anew. A few lines before, he had written, however, that each life plays the same three acts in the human comedy. "The first act is the imagining of the place where contentment exists and may be come to; and the second act reveals the striving toward, and the third act the falling short of, that shining goal, or else (the difference here being negligible) the attaining

of it, to discover that happiness, after all, abides a
thought farther down the bogged, rocky, clogged, befogged,
heart-breaking road, if anywhere."[33] It is these last lines
which render the comoedic metaphor suspect, for in 1932 in
a short sketch called "The Journey," he deplored in about as
tragic a lament as has ever been written the fact that man
and his works are destined to be swept "pell-mell into the
dim incoherency, everywhere a-glitter with their scattered
tinsels."[34]

As late as <u>Smirt</u>, <u>Smith</u>, and <u>Smire</u>, which were published
in 1934, 1935, and 1937, respectively, he still retained much
of his tragic outlook on life. In this microbiography, in
which the life of an individual is set against the macrobi-
ography of the life of Manuel (a biography of corporate man)
like the point within the circle of the cabalists (a word
which closely resembles Cabell's own name, as he must certainly have detected), he set forth each of the three acts
of man. In each of the three acts, the protagonists wear
the front of a smile, as is indicated by the first three
letters of the name of each, but behind the sunny, gallant
façades of all three there is something which belies surface
appearances. The young man's name shades off to <u>Smirt</u>,
suggesting both "smart" and "smirk," for Smirt is a smart
young Alec who smirks and dares to speak condescendingly even
to God himself. Then Smirt is suddenly drawn up short in
<u>Smith</u>, when the young god is already becoming something of
a myth and when he has to become matter-of-fact and pithy.
He enters upon the prosaic middle part of life when he must
perforce become as commonplace as his name and indistinguish-
able from all of the other gray, busy men who go about their
daily routines to earn livings for their families. Then,
the last act is <u>Smire</u>. Although he still wears the <u>Smi-</u> of
<u>smile</u> as jauntily as a cocked hat, yet Smire must willy-
nilly go down into the <u>mire</u>, which contains in it <u>ire</u>. No
matter how much he may <u>rail</u>, or no matter how little he may
complain, he, like all other living creatures, must go down
into the dark cave of Clioth--probably a blend of <u>Clio</u> (the
muse of history) and <u>death</u>. He must, at his death, become
merely a matter of <u>history</u>, as had all other people before
him, such as Jurgen's father, the uncouth old Goth, Coth
(again probably a blend of <u>Clio</u>, <u>death</u>, and <u>Goth</u>). In the
last analysis, then, the individual must be swept back into
the mud, "sans teeth, sans eyes, sans taste, sans everything."
and "thus ends this strange eventful history."

Is this life and this oblivion a tragedy or a comedy?
The answer depends upon the point of view of the beholder.
Cabell himself tried to put a brave front on life, as good

Southerners have always done, after the humiliation and defeat of the War between the States. Cabell had grown up in an atmosphere in which it was second nature to make the best of a bad situation, and so it was only proper that he should don the mask of comedy to hide his heartache and despair. In fact, he wore the mask so continually that he accomplished for himself what he said human beings have always done. By his own imaginings he had brought about, in his own mind, at least, "what ought to be" rather than what perhaps is. By adopting the comic mask he had, through his own romance, given his tragedies the illusion of being comedies, and yet the death's head was constantly lurking behind the smile of the mountebank. He had himself woven little cobwebs of hypocrisies [37] about his own thought, as he said men have always done; he had succeeded in cushioning his own mind against the blow of the grim executioner of all living things. "Mundus vult decipi."

NOTES

[1] *Jesting Moses: A Study in Cabellian Humor* (Gainesville: University of Florida Press, 1962), p. 136.

[2] See, for example, Paul Robert, *Dictionnaire alphabétique et analogique de la langue française*, secrétaire général de rédaction, Alain Ray (Paris: Société du nouveau Littré, 1967), p. 306. This dictionary gives as its first definition of une comédie, "Toute une pièce de théâtre," and then provides as an example, "Racine a fait une pièce qui s'appelle Bajazet." Since Bajazet is a tragedy, the word comédie can obviously be used to mean a play of any kind. Since Cabell had been a French major at William and Mary and since, during his undergraduate days, he had taught some French at this college, he was probably aware of this early use of the word comédie.

[3] William Shakespeare, *As You Like It*, Act II, scene 7, ll. 137-140.

[4] Cabell, *From the Hidden Way*, Works, XIII, 122.

[5] Cabell, *Figures of Earth*, Works, II, 4.

[6] Cabell, *The High Place*, Works, VIII, 238-241. Some critics have said that geas is an anagram for ages, but Julius Rothman has pointed out that the word in Gaelic means "oath" or "vow" and that it can also mean a "prohibition" or "taboo," explanations which, with their various shades of meaning, accord well with the theme of the novel. See Julius Rothman," A Glossarial Index to the 'Biography of the Life of Manuel,'" unpublished Ph.D. dissertation (Columbia, 1954), pp. 167-168. Cabell, as usual, is probably using the term with several different connotations in mind.

[7] See, for example, Cabell, *Figures of Earth*, Works, II, 46-47.

[8] Cabell, *Something About Eve*, Works, X, 311.

[9] Cabell, *Let Me Lie*, pp. 181-199.

[10] Cabell, *Straws and Prayer-Books*, Works, XVII, 238.

[11] Ibid., pp. 272-273.

[12] Alexander Pope, *An Essay on Man*, Epistle II, ll. 217-224.

[13] Cabell, *The Silver Stallion*, Works, III, 205.

[14] Gustave Flaubert, *Emma Bovary*, trans. Eleanor Marx-Aveling (New York: Pocket Books, 1958), p. 66.

[15] Cabell, *Straws and Prayer-Books*, *Works*, XVII, 168.
[16] *Ibid.*, p. 169.
[17] Blaise Pascal, "Pensée 434," *Pensées*, trans. and intro. by A. J. Krailsheimer (Baltimore, Md.: Penguin Books, Inc., 1966), p. 165.
[18] Cabell, *Straws and Prayer-Books*, *Works*, XII, 169.
[19] *Ibid.*, p. xviii.
[20] Cabell, *The Silver Stallion*, *Works*, III, 207-208.
[21] Cabell, *Straws and Prayer-Books*, *Works*, XVII, 26.
[22] *Ibid.*
[23] *Ibid.*, p. 34.
[24] *Ibid.*, p. 23. Also Friedrich Schiller, "Über den Grund des Vergnügens an Tragischen Gegenständen," *Philosophische Briefe, Gesammelte Werke* (n. p.: Sigbert Mohn Verlag, 1960), V, 181-182.
[25] Cabell, *Quiet, Please*, pp. 46-47.
[26] Cabell, *The High Place*, *Works*, VIII, 238-241.
[27] Cabell, *Figures of Earth*, *Works*, II, 58. See, also, *The Silver Stallion*, *Works*, III, 121.
[28] Cabell, *Beyond Life*, *Works*, I, 171-172.
[29] *Ibid.*, pp. x-xi.
[30] *Ibid.*, p. 270.
[31] Cabell, *Quiet, Please*, p. 40.
[32] *Ibid.*
[33] Cabell, *The Lineage of Lichfield*, *Works*, XVI, 254-255.
[34] Cabell, "The Journey," *Richmond Times-Dispatch*, January 31, 1932, Section III, Part 2, p. 2.
[35] Cabell, *Beyond Life*, *Works*, I, 171.